PLAYING THE CARDS

developing competence at the bridge table

By
Norma Sands

First Edition, 1984
Second Printing, March 1988
Manufactured in the United States of America

Copyright © 1984 by
Rocky Mountain Books Co.
Denver, Colorado

Published by
Rocky Mountain Books Co.
Post Office Box 10663
Denver Colorado 80210

ISBN: 0-9605648-7-X

TO
Andrew Brustuen
everyone should have one like him

with appreciation to
Jan Janitschke, Steve Haines & Paul Ossip
and other supportive friends
Anita, Anne, Broma Lou, Don, Georgette, Jerry, Korene,
Laurie, Mary Anne, & Pat

TABLE OF CONTENTS

Part One—Basics of Card Play

I.	Developing Tricks with Secondary Honors	3
II.	Developing Tricks with Long Suits	11
III.	Counting Losers	19
IV.	Eliminating Losers	25
V.	Third Hand Play	31
VI.	Second Hand Play	39

Part Two—For the More Advanced Player

VII.	Trump Management	43
	cross-ruff	
	loser on loser	
	dummy reversal	
	trump coup	
VIII.	Timing and Entries	51
	planning ahead	
	ruffing finesse	
IX.	Playing in the Real World	59
	hold up	
	dangerous opponent	
	ruffing finesse	
	counting the hand	
	backward finesse	
X.	Defensive Signaling	69
	attitude	
	count	
	suit preference	
XI.	Playing it Safe	77
XII.	Playing with Your Opponent's Help	87
	end play/throw-in	
	stripping the hand	
XIII.	Introduction to Squeezes	95
	simple/single	
	double	
	threat cards	
	psuedo squeeze	
	rectifying the count	
	vienna coup	
XIV.	Test Yourself	103

Table 1	Table of Opening Leads	122
Table 2	Table of Percentages	124

PREFACE

Don't you wish you knew how they do it? Those players who seemingly without effort reduce your aces to deuces, turn their spot cards into controls, and systematically beat you like the proverbial drum? When you know you're as bright as they are, as well educated, and a better person besides? Why is it you always feel undergunned? In your depression (and bridge poverty) you suspect not only that they think better than you do, have fewer financial/personal problems than you do, but they probably dabble in black magic and gamble their souls in order to keep on winning.

The horrid truth is that you probably are undergunned. They play with greater skill and so of course win more often. What then to do? How are you to learn to play better bridge (which is probably the only practical solution to losing to these people)?

Fortunately Norma has written a book to help you attain a higher level of skill by teaching you to think more clearly about the game. A little effort and time spent with these pages and you will find yourself practicing a little magic of your own. Instead of shredding dummies, you'll learn to stroke them, instead of cringing on defense, you'll attack with moderate but justifiable confidence, and in general, experience the joy of seeing not only your game improve, but even more importantly, your score.

Now, thanks to Norma, you have the means to put yourself on the winning track.—*Suzanne Jones*

I

DEVELOPING TRICKS WITH SECONDARY HONORS

In most beginning texts on card play, it is recommended that you count winners in a no-trump contract and losers in a suit contract. However, it is not intuitive to a new player to assess how many tricks a given suit is likely to yield. Until one develops this ability, counting a complete hand leads to confusion. Studying suit combinations will help one to assess the hand and subsequently to develop a plan. Although there are limitless combinations, most of them will repeat the same principles.

With the following examples, decide how to play each of the card combinations to take the number of tricks listed. Although this exercise will be useful for suit contracts as well, assume the contract is no-trump. Under each combination is listed the number of tricks you are attempting to take. You can lead from whichever hand you choose, as entries to either hand are readily available. The opponents are presumed to make whatever play is best for their side.

	1.	2.	3.	4.	5.	6.
(Dummy)	A K J	A 3 2	Q 5 4	K Q 4	A J 10	A J 4
(Hand)	3 2	Q J 10	A 6 2	7 6	8 7 6	K 5 3
	Three tricks	Three tricks	Two tricks	Two tricks	Two tricks	Three tricks

	7.	8.	9.	10.	11.	12.
(Dummy)	A 5 4	A Q 10	K 5 4	Q J 2	K J 10	K J 5
(Hand)	K J 10	5 4 3	Q 10 6	A 5 4	5 4 2	4 3 2
	Three tricks	Two tricks	Two tricks	Two tricks	Two tricks	One trick

1. This is a straight finesse. Lead low from hand and if West plays low, try the jack. You have a 50/50 chance of success.
2. Lead the queen intending to play low from dummy if West plays low. If he "covers" your queen with the king, win with the ace. Your jack and ten are then high. Another 50/50 proposition.

3. This is often confused with the last example. Leading the queen here is a losing play. Whoever has the king will play it, giving you no chance to win a trick with the queen. Since you have no backers, you have promoted nothing. The only hope of getting a trick with the queen is by leading low from hand, hoping the king is on the left. If West takes the king, your queen will later take a trick. If West plays low, you must play your queen as this is your only chance for a trick. 50/50 chance.

4. Lead from your hand toward the king-queen. If LHO (left hand opponent) plays low, play an honor. If it loses to the ace, you get only one trick; but if it wins, get back to the bottom hand with another suit and repeat. You win two tricks whenever the ace is on your left. 50/50.

5. Lead from the bottom hand and assuming LHO plays low, play the ten. If this loses to the king or queen, get back to your hand with another suit and lead towards the jack. The likelihood of getting two tricks is 75%. Look at the possibilities:

Left:	Right:
1. K	Q
2. Q	K
3. K Q	—
4. —	K Q

Only case four loses both times. Three of the four cases produce two tricks.

6. Leading up to the jack is the best chance of gaining a third trick. Playing the king first is okay, but leading the jack towards the king is a no-win play because you don't have the ten. This would be the same error as leading the queen in example three.

7. In this example you have an option, because you have both the jack and the ten. You can finesse either opponent. If you think the queen is on your right, lead from dummy towards the jack-ten. If you think the queen is on your left, lead the jack or ten intending to let it ride if it's not covered. With no clues in the bidding, the best play is to lead the jack. If it's not covered, assume West doesn't have the queen and play the ace, then lead back toward the 10 and finesse it if RHO plays low.

8. Lead from the bottom hand and insert the ten. If this loses to the king, you have two tricks. If it loses to the jack, come back to the bottom hand and finesse the queen. This suit has a 75% chance for two tricks. On a bad day both finesses lose. On a good day, with both the king and jack "on side" (favorably located), you will win all three tricks.

9. Lead low towards the king. Whether this wins or loses, as soon as you are able, lead low from dummy and finesse the ten. You win two tricks anytime the jack is in the East hand. Also you would have two tricks if West makes the error of playing the ace as you lead low to the king. (Second hand play is covered in Chapter VI.)

10. Lead the queen. If it's covered with the king, play the ace, and your jack is good. Notice that if the finesse loses, you have two tricks; if the finesse wins, you still have only two tricks. The only advantage to the king being on side is that you can come to two tricks without giving up the lead. With some hands this may be important.

11. Lead low from hand, playing the jack or ten if LHO plays low. If this wins or forces the ace, go back to your hand with another suit and repeat the finesse. You will win two tricks whenever the queen is on your left. You may have noticed by now, that the ten has very little value on its own, but it often increases your trick taking potential when it's with other honors.

12. Lead towards the jack. If it loses to the queen, get back to your hand and lead towards the king. If both the ace and queen are on your right, you get no tricks. If both are on your left you get two tricks. If the honors are divided, which is more likely than either of the other two conditions, you will get one trick. There is a 75% chance of at least one trick.

Left:	Right:
1. —	A Q
2. A Q	—
3. A	Q
4. Q	A

Now for some hands. You are declarer in a no-trump contract on all of the following hands:

Hand #1

North
♠ A 6 4
♥ Q 5 4
♦ A 8 4
♣ J 10 5 4

West   East

South
♠ K 7 3
♥ A 3 2
♦ 10 3 2
♣ A K Q 7

CONTRACT: 3NT
OPENING LEAD: ♠2

COUNT YOUR TOP WINNERS, meaning tricks that could be taken anytime without having to lose the lead. You have two spades, one heart, one diamond, and four clubs. This is only eight winnters, so you need to develop one more. If the heart king is on your left, you can get a trick with the heart queen. Win the spade in your hand with the king and lead a heart towards dummy, planning to play the queen if LHO plays small. (You could play the clubs first if you choose, but the heart play must be made while you have the spade and diamond suits still in control.) If LHO plays the heart king, your queen will be good later. You can win anything he returns and take your nine tricks.

Leading a heart towards your queen will work anytime the heart king is on your left. If it is not...nobody said you would make all your contracts.

THE WHOLE HAND

North
♠ A 6 4
♥ Q 5 4
♦ A 8 4
♣ J 10 5 4

West
♠ Q 10 8 2
♥ K 9 6
♦ K 7 5
♣ 9 8 2

East
♠ J 9 5
♥ J 10 8 7
♦ Q J 9 6
♣ 6 3

South
♠ K 7 3
♥ A 3 2
♦ 10 3 2
♣ A K Q 7

Hand #2

North
- ♠ A J 10
- ♥ 8 5 2
- ♦ 9 8 7
- ♣ A 10 9 2

West   **East**

South
- ♠ 4 3 2
- ♥ K 7 6 4
- ♦ A K
- ♣ K Q J 4

THE AUCTION:

South	West	North	East
1NT	Pass	3NT	Pass
Pass	Pass		

OPENING LEAD: ♥3

We assume LHO to have exactly four hearts. Dummy has the two, so the three is the lowest heart outstanding. If the opponents lead fourth best, West cannot have a five card suit. You have four top clubs, two top diamonds, and one top spade. That's seven tricks, plus a heart trick which will be coming to you soon, so you need one more trick. Suppose RHO plays the heart jack at trick one and you win with your king. Now what?

You can see your only chance for an extra trick is in the spade suit. Tackle it now, while you still have plenty of entries and have control of the rest of the suits. At trick two, lead a spade to the ten. If this loses, the opponents will probably cash three heart tricks. Whatever they return, you can win and repeat the spade finesse. You will make two spade tricks any time West has at least one spade honor.

North
♠ 8 4 3
♥ K 5
♦ 8 7 6 2
♣ K Q 4 3

West
♠ J 7 6
♥ 8 7
♦ A J 9 5 3
♣ 7 6 2

East
♠ K Q 10
♥ Q 10 9 6 2
♦ Q
♣ 10 9 8 5

South
♠ A 9 5 2
♥ A J 4 3
♦ K 10 4
♣ A J

THE AUCTION:

South	*West*	*North*	*East*
1NT	Pass	2NT	Pass
3NT	Pass	Pass	Pass

OPENING LEAD: ♦ 5

In all cases where all four hands are shown, cover the East-West hands as you analyze the hand. Your winners include one in spades, two in hearts, and four in clubs. With the diamond king, the total is eight. A successful heart finesse would do it. You play a low diamond from dummy, East plays the queen, and you win with the king. You must lead from the board for the heart finesse, but before doing that you need to play the ace and jack of clubs because the club suit is "blocked" (meaning you can't cash it without using another suit for transportation). After cashing the ace and jack of clubs, go to the board with the heart king and play the king and queen of clubs. Now lead a heart to the jack. When this wins you are home.

Although the above example contained a suit that needed the use of another suit for an entry to cash all of the tricks, new players have been known to bungle one like the following:

Dummy
A J 3 2

Hand
K Q 4

If one were to play the ace first, another suit would be needed in order to cash four tricks. If there doesn't happen to be another entry to the upper hand, the jack is lost. The problem easily can be avoided by playing the high honors in the shorter hand first.

II

DEVELOPING TRICKS
WITH LONG SUITS

It's possible to develop extra winners not only with secondary honors, as in the last chapter, but also with long suits. Determine what division of the opponents' cards will allow you take the number of tricks listed:

1.	2.	3.	4.	5.	6.
A Q 4 3	A K 4 3 2	A 8 5 4 3	A 7 5 3 2	A K 4 3	A 8 7 6 4
K 5 2	Q 6 5	K 6 2	K 6	8 7 6 2	K 5 3 2
Four tricks	Five tricks	Four tricks	Four tricks	Three tricks	Five tricks

1. You will win four tricks any time the suit breaks 3-3, which will occur about 36% of the time. Try to weed out of your vocabulary expressions like "even splits". If you think in specific terms like a 3-3 break, it is easy to count. When you play the king and both follow, that's one. When you play the queen if both follow that's two. Finally, as you play the ace, if both follow you have the 3-3 break, so your last card is good. You have found out by counting to three, which is how experts count. This is much more efficient than adding each time and counting to 13.
2. You have eight cards, so you are missing only five. Odds favor a 3-2 break, so you rate to take five tricks.
3. Once again you have eight cards, but this time you have only two of the top winners. With a normal break (3-2), you will have to lose one, but will then have four winners.
4. You have seven cards in this suit. If the remaining six cards are 3-3, you could play the king, then ace, then lose a trick (or king, then lose a trick, then ace). If both opponents followed to all three rounds, you have a 3-3 break and your last two cards are good. It's more realistic, however, to expect three tricks with this holding. With a more typical 4-2 break, it would necessitate giving the opponents two tricks to develop a third trick.

Example: A 7 5 3 2

West   East

10 8   Q J 9 4

K 6

5. This is a variation of number three. With a 3-2 break you will lose one trick and win three.
6. You will win five tricks when the four missing cards are divided 2-2. The distribution is more likely to be 3-1, however, so this suit will produce four winners more often than five. An easy memory aid on missing cards is that even numbers don't tend to split perfectly, and odd numbers tend to break as evenly as possible. (See percentage table).

Time for a hand. You are in three no-trump, with a lead of the four spades:

Hand #1

North
- ♠ 7 6
- ♥ 7 5 3
- ♦ A K 6 4 3
- ♣ 7 6 5

West
- ♠ K J 9 4 2
- ♥ Q J 8 4
- ♦ 10 8
- ♣ 10 2

East
- ♠ 10 5 3
- ♥ 10 9 6
- ♦ Q J 9
- ♣ Q J 9 8

South
- ♠ A Q 8
- ♥ A K 2
- ♦ 7 5 2
- ♣ A K 4 3

CONTRACT: 3NT
OPENING LEAD: ♠4

With a spade lead you can count two top spades as you are getting a free finesse. You also have two top tricks in hearts, diamonds and clubs which totals eight. With your long diamond suit, this should be an easy hand. It's only easy if you recognize that you must lose a diamond in order to take more than two tricks in the suit. Since you have no entries to dummy outside of the diamond suit, it is essential to give up a diamond sometime prior to playing the ace and king. If you play the ace and king and then lose one, you will be unable to get back to dummy to cash your two winners. **As a general rule, when it is *certain* that you have to lose a trick in a suit before you can win the tricks you expect, lose the trick as soon as possible.** The old axiom, "Take your losses early", is too general. Rather, give up a trick when the *purpose* is to develop extra winners. So, after winning the spade lead, play a low diamond from each hand and the rest will be easy.

Hand #2

North
♠ A Q 3 2
♥ 9 4
♦ J 10 4 3
♣ K 6 4

West
♠ 9 8 7
♥ Q 10 8 6 3
♦ A 9 5
♣ Q 8

East
♠ K J 6
♥ J 7 5 2
♦ 7
♣ J 10 9 7 5

South
♠ 10 5 4
♥ A K
♦ K Q 8 6 2
♣ A 3 2

THE AUCTION:

South	West	North	East
1NT	Pass	2C	Pass
2D	Pass	3NT	Pass

OPENING LEAD: ♥6

You have five top winners. Taking the spade finesse would be a silly play as you don't need it. By driving out the ace of diamonds there are four certain diamond tricks, which added to your five top winners guarantees your contract. Notice what would happen if you finessed the spade. East would win and return a heart. Now when West wins the diamond, you will go down. Take a finesse when you need it, not just because it's there.

The following suits have length as well as some secondary honors. Think through how you would go about trying to get the number of tricks listed:

1.	2.	3.	4.	5.	6.
J32	AJ32	AJ32	AQ43	K742	AQ43
AK754	K876	K8654	J762	Q653	J109762
Five tricks	Four tricks	Five tricks	Four tricks	Three tricks	Six tricks

7.
AQ93

J76542

Six
tricks

1. By now you should know not to lead the jack, since you don't have the ten (see ex. 3 in Chapter I). Play the ace and king. Your only hope for five tricks is if the queen is doubleton. If percentages are of interest to you, a 3-2 break will occur about 68% of the time. Of the 3-2 breaks, the queen will be in the hand with two cards two of the five times, or 40%. The likelihood of five tricks, therefore, is 40% of 68%, or about 27%. Having this exact information may not be necessary, but many people who enjoy bridge also enjoy this kind of thinking. If you're not one of them, ignore this last part.

2. Play the king and if both follow small, lead low towards the jack for a finesse. With five cards missing, the most likely break is 3-2. The queen will be doubleton *less* than half of the time, where as the finesse is exactly half.

3. Having nine cards, it is slightly better to play the two top honors rather than to finesse. You will win all of the tricks whenever the suit is 2-2 and whenever the queen is singleton.

4. The only holding that will allow you to win four tricks is a doubleton king on side. Lead low to the queen for a finesse and if it wins play the ace.

5. Lead low from either hand towards the king or queen. If it wins, play low from both hands, at trick two, hoping for a doubleton ace. If your king or queen were to be captured by the ace, you would have to lose two tricks.

6. You have ten cards. Suppose you lead the jack from the lower hand and LHO plays low. The question is whether to finesse or play the ace, hoping the king will fall. Look at the table showing every possible holding:

Left:	Right:	
K	8 5	Cannot missguess
5	K 8	Both plays lose
8	K 5	Both plays lose
—	K 8 5	Both plays lose
K 8	5	Finesse Wins
K 5	8	Finesse Wins
K 8 5	—	Finesse Wins
8 5	K	Playing the ace Wins

The finesse is clearly the better play.

7. As illustrated in the last example, it is clearly right to finesse for the king. If you lead low and finesse the queen and RHO shows out, you can no longer avoid losing a trick to west's K 10. You should lead the jack (without the ten you say!). It's time you find out that almost everything in bridge has an exception or two. If you lead the jack and LHO covers, when East shows out, you come back to your hand and take the marked finesse against the ten.

On the following hand you are declarer in four hearts:

Hand #3

North
♠ 8 5 2
♥ K 7 5 2
♦ A K 3
♣ Q J 3

South
♠ 7 4
♥ Q 8 6 3
♦ Q J 10 4
♣ A K 2

THE AUCTION:

South	West	North	East
1D	1S	Double*	Pass
2H	Pass	4H	Pass
Pass	Pass		

*Negative

OPENING LEAD: ♠K

The king of spades is followed by the jack of spades, and on the third round East plays the ace as you trump. You have lost two tricks and can lose only one heart. LHO over-called one spade and didn't have the ace. Your best hope is that he has the doubleton ace of hearts. Lead a low heart to the king and if that holds, play a low heart from dummy, playing low from your hand.

West's Hand:
♠ K Q J 10 3
♥ A 4
♦ 8 6
♣ 10 8 6 4

Hand #4

North
♠ 8 7 2
♥ 6 2
♦ A 7 6 3
♣ K J 4 2

South
♠ A Q 4
♥ K 7 4
♦ K Q 2
♣ A 7 5 3

THE AUCTION:

South	West	North	East
1NT	Pass	2NT	Pass
3NT	Pass	Pass	Pass

OPENING LEAD: ♥5

You have three top diamonds, two clubs, and one spade, plus as it happens, you win the opening lead with the king of hearts which makes seven winners. There are possibilities for extra tricks in every suit except hearts. It is usually best to tackle the long one first, so at trick two, play the ace of clubs followed by a low club to the jack. That wins, but East shows out so you have only three club tricks. You need to find one more trick for your contract. You could lead a low spade towards your hand and finesse the queen, or the diamond suit could be 3-3. Which do you do?

Play the king and queen of diamonds (playing the high honors in the short hand first), followed by a low diamond to the ace. If the diamonds break 3-3, you have nine tricks; if not, try the spade finesse. This gives you two chances for your contract instead of putting all of your eggs in one basket. (The heart suit happens to be divided 4-4, but you don't know that.)

THE WHOLE HAND

North
- ♠ 8 7 2
- ♥ 6 2
- ♦ A 7 6 3
- ♣ K J 4 2

West
- ♠ K 9
- ♥ A J 9 5
- ♦ 10 8 4
- ♣ Q 10 8 6

East
- ♠ J 10 6 5 3
- ♥ Q 10 8 3
- ♦ J 9 5
- ♣ 9

South
- ♠ A Q 4
- ♥ K 7 4
- ♦ K Q 2
- ♣ A 7 5 3

III

COUNTING LOSERS

Counting losers is a quick way of assessing what problems must be dealt with in a suit contract. With some hands it may be helpful to count winners as well, but since you have to get the hand played sometime during the course of the evening, let's consider one thing at a time.

In the following exercise, you are in a trump contract and this is one of your side suits which was *not* led on the opening lead. Count the losers in each example, assuming you will have to lead the suit at some point. You have plenty of trump in each hand.

1.	2.	3.	4.	5.	6.
872	72	9	Q64	J52	A542
AK5	AK5	1052·	873	Q73	K876

7.	8.	9.	10.	11.	12.
K2	AQ	Q54	KQ4	A54	A8632
74	6	A72	863	102	K94

13.	14.	15.	16.
J64	KJ6	K32	QJ4
AQ3	752	Q64	876

1. One loser.
2. No losers. The third round could be trumped in dummy.
3. One loser. Dummy can trump after the first round.
4. Three losers. Only on a very good day will the queen win a trick. Usually it will be captured by an opponent's ace or king.
5. Probably three losers. When you play low to the jack, the second hand to play usually will play low, since his partner is in a position to capture the jack. When you lead from dummy and play the queen, it will probably be captured by the remaining honor. Only when both honors are in the same hand are you favored to win a trick, and both are probably not in the opening leader's hand. Holding the ace and king, West normally would have led the king.
6. With a 3-2 break (most likely), you will lose one trick. With a 4-1 break or a 5-0 break, two tricks.
7. One or two losers, depending on which opponent has the ace.

8. No losers. Unless the hand is such that you must win a trick with the queen to make your contract, you will not take the finesse.

9. One or two losers. You will lead towards the queen in dummy, hoping the king is on your left.

10. One or two losers, depending on who has the ace.

11. One loser. You can trump the third round.

12. One loser. If you get a bad break you still have only one loser, but would have fewer winners in the suit.

13. One loser. Usually you will lose a trick to the king whether it's on side or off side. The king doubleton on side or a singleton king are the only legitimate holdings to have no losers, and those holdings are unlikely.

14. Probably two losers. You expect to take a trick with one of your honors by leading towards them. See #12 in Chapter I.

15. Two losers. Usually one of your honors will be captured by the ace. This would leave you with one winner and two losers.

16. Most often two losers. You can lead towards the queen/jack twice. Only when both the ace and king are on your right will you lose all three tricks.

Count the losers in a complete hand:

Hand #1

North
- ♠ A 5 4 3
- ♥ A 5 3
- ♦ 4 5
- ♣ 8 7 5 4

South
- ♠ K 8 7 6 2
- ♥ K 4
- ♦ A K 6
- ♣ A 3 2

CONTRACT: 4 ♠
OPENING LEAD: ♥Q

The trumps could be divided 3-1, 2-2, or 4-0. Since 3-1 is most likely, it's reasonable to expect one trump loser, no heart or diamond losers, and two club losers. Pull two rounds of trump and unless you find a 4-0 break you will make your contract.

North
♠ 9 8 5
♥ 7 5 4 2
♦ J
♣ A 8 7 6 5

South
♠ A K 7 4 2
♥ A K 3
♦ A 6 3
♣ J 2

CONTRACT: 4 ♠
OPENING LEAD: ♣K

You can't escape a trump loser and you have to lose one heart and one club. What about diamonds? There are no diamond losers provided that you trump them. Notice that dummy has only three trump. If you were to play two rounds of trump, dummy could no longer ruff both of your small diamonds. The best play is to win the club lead with the ace followed by the ace of diamonds and ruff a diamond. Next, lead a trump to your king and trump your last diamond. Now get back to your hand with a heart and play the ace of trump. This is an example of the most valid reason to delay pulling trump—a short suit in dummy, and dummy having only three trump.

Count your losers on the next hand and plan your play:

Hand #3

North
- ♠ J 3 2
- ♥ 8 6 2
- ♦ K J 8 6 5
- ♣ 7 5

West
- ♠ 10 8 7 5
- ♥ J 4
- ♦ Q 10 4 3
- ♣ K J 9

East
- ♠ K 9 4
- ♥ 9 7 3
- ♦ A 9
- ♣ Q 10 8 3 2

South
- ♠ A Q 6
- ♥ A K Q 10 5
- ♦ 7 2
- ♣ A 6 4

THE AUCTION:

South	West	North	East
1H	Pass	2H	Pass
4H	Pass	Pass	Pass

OPENING LEAD: ♦3

Probably no trump losers, one spade loser, at least one diamond loser, and one club loser—**provided** that you trump a club before pulling trumps.

First things first. Against a suit contract, it is very dangerous to lead low from a suit containing an ace because if declarer wins the trick and either declarer or dummy had a singleton, the ace never takes a trick. Most people know this, so at trick one try the jack from dummy. If this forces the ace, you are in good position. Suppose East wins the ace and returns a diamond. After winning the king, play the ace of clubs and a low club, preparing to trump a club in dummy. Your contract should now be safe. Notice it would have been okay to play one round of trumps first, but if you played two rounds, the opponents could play another trump when they win the club. Dummy would then be out of trump and you would lose two club tricks.

North
- ♠ 7 6 2
- ♥ 6 5
- ♦ A K 4 3
- ♣ 9 6 5 2

West
- ♠ Q 9 4
- ♥ Q 8 2
- ♦ 10 5
- ♣ K Q J 4 3

East
- ♠ J 10
- ♥ A K J 10 7
- ♦ 9 8 7
- ♣ 10 8 7

South
- ♠ A K 8 5 3
- ♥ 9 4 3
- ♦ Q J 6 2
- ♣ A

CONTRACT: 4 ♠
OPENING LEAD: ♣K

Usually you will lose one trump trick, two or three heart tricks, no diamonds, and no clubs. Plan your play.

Here it is again; unless you trump a heart in dummy, you will lose three heart tricks. Play a heart at trick two. When you gain the lead again, play another heart. This kind of situation occurs so often it's worth noticing.

If you are thinking about losers, your loser count is reduced from three heart losers to two. Another way of looking at it is that your trumps are **extended**. Most likely, you will win four trump tricks in your hand. If you trump once in dummy, you extend your trump tricks to five.

Follow the play of the next hand to see what went wrong:

Hand #5

North
♠ K 6 5 4
♥ 4
♦ 9 7 5
♣ Q J 10 5 3

West
♠ Q 9 3
♥ K Q 10 6 2
♦ 4 3
♣ A 8 7

East
♠ J 10 8 7
♥ J 9 8 3
♦ 10 8 2
♣ K 6

South
♠ A 2
♥ A 7 5
♦ A K Q J 6
♣ 9 4 2

CONTRACT: 5 ♦
OPENING LEAD: ♥K

Declarer won the opening heart lead and trumped a heart. Next he played the ace and king of spades and trumped a spade. He then trumped his last heart and pulled trump in three rounds. He then led a club toward dummy. East won and returned a heart which declarer trumped with his last trump. When he led another club, West won and cashed a heart for the setting trick. What did declarer do wrong?

One of the most common errors new players make in playing trump contracts is to arrange to trump in the hand which is long in trump. Whereas it extends your trumps to trump in the short hand (which is more often dummy), it usually does not gain to set out to trump in the hand with length in trump. In cases such as this last hand, it can ruin you.

Declarer should win the ace of hearts and trump a heart. Then he should get back to his hand with a trump and ruff the last heart. Now he should lead a spade to his hand and pull trump. He will have two trumps left so he can knock out the ace and king of clubs and keep control of the hand.

The term "cross-ruff" is often used by inexperienced players, although the true cross-ruff hand comes up only rarely. When declarer regards a hand such as the last hand as a cross-ruff, he can run into trouble. Repeated exposure to this is believed to have shortened the lives of many bridge instructors. A cross-ruff hand is shown in a later chapter on trump management.

IV

ELIMINATING LOSERS

After counting losers, what do you do when there are too many? Occasionally you are in a contract that simply cannot make, in which case it's best to avoid agonizing and get on to the next hand. Much of the time however, if you take a few seconds to look over the hand, there is a play which offers you a possibility of making your contract. One of the ways you can make losers disappear is to discard them on your winners (which you may have to establish).

Hand #1

North
♠ J 8 3 2
♥ 8 7 6
♦ A K J
♣ K J 3

South
♠ Q 10 9 5 4
♥ A 5 3
♦ 6 4
♣ A Q 7

CONTRACT: 4 ♠
OPENING LEAD: ♥ 2

You have four losers, the ace and king of trump and two hearts. Plan your play.

A typical play by a beginner would be as follows: starting at trick two, the king of diamonds, the ace of diamonds and trump a diamond. This is a spinning-your-wheels play. The same four losers are still there, so the problem is ignored.

By now you have probably figured out the correct play. At trick two you must finesse the diamond jack. If it loses you will go down two, but if it wins you are on your way to making your contract. On the third diamond you will discard a heart, thus eliminating a loser.

People often worry about someone trumping the third diamond. It is unlikely as you held only five diamonds between your hand and dummy. You should worry about opponents ruffing your long suits, not the short suits. Besides, it's your only real hope to make the contract. Notice in this hand that the loser must be eliminated before touching trump as the trump suit is missing the top honors and the heart suit is wide open.

Plan your play on the following hand with three different opening leads:

Hand #2

North
- ♠ 8 7 3 2
- ♥ A Q
- ♦ K Q J 2
- ♣ 5 4 3

South
- ♠ A 9 6 5 4
- ♥ 3
- ♦ A 9 6 4
- ♣ A 9 6

THE AUCTION:

West	North	East	South
	1D	Pass	1S
Pass	2S	Pass	4S
Pass	Pass	Pass	

OPENING LEAD:
    Case A: ♦ 3
    Case B: ♥ 5
    Case C: ♣ K

A. You have one or two trump losers (if they are 4-0 it's time to go to the next hand), and two club losers. Since you still have the club ace you are in no hurry to eliminate a club loser. Instead, you should play the ace and another trump as you are worried about a diamond ruff. If trumps are 2-2, you are home. If not, you will need the heart finesse.

B. This is a freebee. Although you didn't count a possible heart loser, finesse the queen. Even if it loses, later you can discard a club on the heart ace. It can't hurt to try the finesse, as it is, at worst, exchanging a loser.

C. An interesting situation. If trumps are 2-2, the heart finesse isn't needed. If you took it and it lost, you would go down as your clubs are wide open. On the other hand, if trumps are 3-1, the heart finesse is your only chance. Since your club ace is dislodged, you can't test trumps, but must commit yourself. (You can play the trump ace, but you are still in the same position). You have nothing to go on except for the odds. A 3-1 trump break is more likely than 2-2 (50% versus 40%) so your best bet is to take the heart finesse, to try to eliminate a club loser.

With the next hand you arrive in four hearts on somewhat meager values. Given the queen of spades lead, the hand is not difficult, but players often get careless with one like this.

Hand #3

North
♠ A K 4
♥ Q 10 7 3
♦ 5 4 3
♣ Q J 2

West
♠ Q J 10 3 2
♥ 9 8
♦ 8 7 2
♣ A 9 8

East
♠ 9 8 7
♥ A
♦ K Q J 10
♣ 10 7 6 5 3

South
♠ 6 5
♥ K J 6 5 4 2
♦ A 9 6
♣ K 4

CONTRACT: 4 ♥
OPENING LEAD: ♠Q

You have four losers, a trump, two diamonds, and a club. One diamond can go on dummy's third club, and you must play the club king right now, because if you lose the lead by playing a trump, the opponents may attack diamonds before you drive out the ace of clubs. Had a diamond been led, you were almost certain to fail. With a spade lead, you have the chance to eliminate a diamond loser on a club.

Some of the more challenging play problems occur when you have bid a bit too much. On the next hand, you are in four spades with the king of clubs led:

Hand #4

North
- ♠ Q 9 4
- ♥ 8 3
- ♦ A K 7 6 2
- ♣ 10 6 5

South
- ♠ A K 8 3 2
- ♥ J 10 9
- ♦ 8 4
- ♣ A 3 2

You have two choices. You can yell at partner for bidding so much or you can try to make the hand. You have two or three heart losers and two club losers. If you try to ruff a heart in dummy, you will avoid three heart losers, but will give yourself no chance for the contract. Your only hope lies in the diamond suit. Play the ace and king of trump, hoping both opponents follow, then play the ace and king of diamonds and trump a diamond. If diamonds split 3-3, play a trump to the queen, and discard your two small clubs on dummy's two diamond winners. You will lose only three heart tricks.

Hand #5

North
- ♠ 5 3
- ♥ 7 6 5
- ♦ 6 4 2
- ♣ A K J 10 2

West
- ♠ 10 4
- ♥ K J 9
- ♦ A K 10 8 3
- ♣ 9 8 5

East
- ♠ Q J 6
- ♥ Q 8 3 2
- ♦ J 9 7 5
- ♣ 7 4

South
- ♠ A K 9 8 7 2
- ♥ A 10 4
- ♦ Q
- ♣ Q 6 3

CONTRACT: 4 ♠
OPENING LEAD: ♦ K

After winning the diamond king, West continues with the ace. There is probably one trump loser, plus one in diamonds and two in hearts. The club suit should absorb a couple of these.

When the ace and king of trumps are played, both follow. Normally it is pointless to play another trump when the only trump outstanding is the highest card; the loser can't be avoided. However, with this hand, it is necessary to play another trump. The reason is that you want to run the clubs and your plans will be thwarted unless the last trump is driven out. East would trump the third club and you would be permanently cut off from dummy's remaining club winners. When you want to run a suit and cannot afford to have it interrupted, it is necessary to drive out the high trump.

V

THIRD HAND PLAY

Defense is the part of the game people find to be most difficult. This chapter will deal with the play problems encountered when partner has led. The next chapter will cover second hand play, and there is a later chapter on defensive signaling.

There are a number of considerations when you are in third position. For example, partner may be leading either high or low, dummy may have honors or small cards, and you may have small cards or more than one honor, etc. Your play normally will be the same versus suit contracts or no trump. Consider first when partner led low at trick one and dummy has small cards. Usually partner will lead a suit that has some potential of developing tricks for your side and you want to help make that happen. Assuming you do not have touching honors, you should play the highest card you have, either to win the trick or force out declarer's top cards, thus establishing winners in partner's hand.

If partner leads the five on the following example, and dummy plays low you must play the queen:

9 4 3

West   East
K 10 7 5 2   Q 8 6

A J

If you play anything else, whether the contract is no-trump or suit, you will give declarer an extra trick.

If, however, you have touching honors such as K Q or Q J 10, the trick taking potential is EQUAL. In this case, play the lower or lowest of your touching honors. Your purpose in playing the lower is to help partner figure out who has what.

For example, partner leads the four of the following suit:

6 5

West   East
K 8 7 4 2   Q J 3

You play the jack and declarer plays the ace. Partner will know you have the queen as well as the jack because declarer wouldn't have spent his ace if he could have won the trick with the queen. It's not always clear exactly what partner has, but if you have this agreement with partner, he will always know that you do **not** hold the honor just below the one you played. Since important information can be passed, this play is standard among virtually all bridge players. Declarer can see both his hands; but defenders cannot see their full arsenal, so have to have ways of communicating information about their hands.

If dummy has an honor, it can affect your play. Suppose partner leads the five of this suit and dummy plays low and you have the following:

Dummy
J 7 2

Partner's lead
5

You
Case A: A 6 4
Case B: Q 10 3
Case C: K Q 4
Case D: A Q 8 6

A. Play the ace, the highest card in partner's suit.
B. Play the ten. It is as effective as the queen since you have the jack surrounded.
C. Play the queen, the lower of your "equal" honors.
D. Play the ace. These honors are not touching.

Dummy
Q 6 4

Partner's lead
3

You
Case A: K J 5
Case B: K J 10
Case C: A J 5

A. Play the jack. You have the queen surrounded.
B. Play the ten. Same as above plus you have touching honors.
C. This situation is a bit more complex. Without the jack, you would, of course, play the ace. Although it is usually correct to play the highest card you have except when your honors are touching, there are exceptions. Here, the play of the jack is correct. Suppose partner led from the king. Your jack will win and your side will collect all of the tricks. Had you played the ace, declarer eventually could take a trick with the queen. If

partner **doesn't** have the king, by playing the ace, you would be establishing both the king and queen for declarer. If you insert the jack, you may be able to capture the queen later.

When partner has led low and you win the trick, you will almost always continue with this suit. The card you select to return is important both for helping to develop tricks for your side and to help partner know what you have in the suit. The following generalization may be helpful: **When you hold three cards in partner's led suit, if your high one wins, return the card that was originally your middle card; with four or five cards in the suit, return the fourth best (which in the case of four would be the lowest card).**

Look first at the situation in which you hold three cards. Partner leads the six of this suit against a three no-trump contract.

Dummy
9 8

K 10 7 6 2   You
                                    A J 3

Q 5 4

Dummy plays small and you win the ace. You must return the jack. If declarer plays the queen, partner wins and takes the next three tricks. If you return the three, look at what happens: Declarer plays the queen and partner the king. The next round of the suit puts the lead in *your* hand. This is what is known as a "blocked" suit. Unless partner has an entry in another suit, the last two winners will never materialize.

Although the last example is more dramatic that most, it is correct to return your middle card from three even when that middle card doesn't seem important. When players begin to watch the small cards as well as the big ones a great deal of information is available. Observe the following hand:

Hand #1

North
♠ 6 3
♥ A 7 4
♦ K 8 2
♣ Q J 10 5 4

West
♠ K J 9 4
♥ 10 8 6 3
♦ 9 7
♣ 8 7 6

East
♠ A 7 2
♥ 9 5
♦ Q J 10 5 3
♣ A 9 2

South
♠ Q 10 8 5
♥ K Q J 2
♦ A 6 4
♣ K 3

THE AUCTION:

South	West	North	East
1NT	Pass	3NT	Pass
Pass	Pass		

West leads the spade four, East wins with the ace and returns the seven. Declarer plays the ten and West the jack. West now must decide if he should cash his king. In this case, it would be a mistake. It would allow declarer to win a trick with the queen and make the contract. West should note that dummy has played the six and the three, while declarer played the five and the ten. The two is still missing. It looks as if partner returned his middle card and still has the two. If partner could get the lead again and lead through declarer's queen, West would get *two* more tricks in the suit.

With the West hand being so weak, it is reasonable to expect that partner has another winner. That other winner plus the four spade tricks would defeat the contract. It takes practice to learn to watch the small cards or "spot cards", but it is not hard to remember to return the (original) middle card, and that is a step in the right direction.

With four cards in the suit, if you win the lead it is best to return your lowest card. Partner can now deduce that you started out with either a doubleton or with four cards. For example:

                              10 2

    K J 8 5 4   A 9 7 3

                               Q 6

West leads the five against 3NT. Partner wins the ace and returns the three as declarer plays the queen and West wins the king. West can see that the three is the lowest card since the two was in dummy. His partner therefore started out with either two or four (sometimes one can tell from the bidding which is more likely). If partner started out with four, his side owns the first five tricks. If partner started out with two, he couldn't return the suit if he got in again. In this case, declarer would have the 9 7 left and West the J 8 4. West will now have to consider the bidding and look at the hand as a whole to make a decision as to what to do. There is an inference that declarer started with a doubleton. Had the original holding been Q 9 7 6, at trick two, he would probably play low since the ten is in dummy.

An exception to returning the lowest card from four is when your two middle cards are big and could block the suit.

                               7 6

    K 9 8 5 2   A J 10 3

                               Q 4

Here, when West leads the five against a no-trump contract, East must win the ace and return the jack. If he were to return the three, after partner wins the king the next two tricks will be won by the East hand. East must avoid blocking the suit.

Versus a *suit* contract, partner will often lead an honor in an attempt to establish winners before declarer or dummy is out of the suit. Suppose partner led the king of hearts (showing that he also has the ace or the queen) against a four spade contract.

Dummy
- ♠ 8 3 2
- ♥ 8 7 6
- ♦ A K 4 3
- ♣ 6 5 4

partner

your heart holding
Case A: 5 4 2
Case B: 9 4
Case C: Q 9 4
Case D: J 10 3 2
Case E: Q 4
Case F: Q J 3

Your job, when partner leads a high card which could win the trick, is to let partner know whether or not your hand is such that you want him to continue the suit. Sometimes partner's holding is such that he will continue regardless of what you play, but other times your help or "attitude" is appreciated. Your lowest card indicates no interest in the suit. When you want partner to continue, play the highest card you can afford.

A. Play the two. You have no interest.
B. Play the nine. Assuming you want to trump the third round, you would want partner to continue.
C. Again, play the nine. Your side may take the first three tricks.
D. Play the two. If partner led from AKx he would create a trick for declarer by continuing.
E. Play the four. You would like for partner to continue but your queen is too valuable a card to sacrifice.
F. Play the queen. Partner must have the ace and king and you want to be sure to get your three top tricks. The queen is such a valuable card that it tells partner you have either a singleton queen or the queen and jack. Partner can safely lead low to the next trick as you will be able to win it.

The type of signaling advocated here is reflecting *attitude* whenever partner leads a high card. This would also be in effect if partner leads low and dummy wins with a high card such as the ace. If you liked partner's lead, try to show it by playing the highest card you can afford such as:

A. 8̲ 2 B. K 9̲ 4 C. K 3̲ 2

Note in the last case, playing the three is the best you can do. Hopefully, partner will note that the deuce did not appear.

In order to defend a hand effectively you need to know your whole hand as well as the entire auction. The above information is to acquaint you with some tools for communicating. It is a start in helping you and partner to visualize what is in the unseen hands.

SECOND HAND PLAY

There is an important distinction in objectives between the second and third hand play. As discussed in the last chapter, partner normally will lead a suit that has a potential of developing winners for your side. Therefore, unless partner has led a high card, in third position you almost always will try to win the trick, or if you can't, you will reflect your attitude about that suit.

When you are in second position, most of the time the suit is *not* one in which your side hopes to develop several tricks, since *declarer* is leading it. Therefore, usually you do not try to win the trick, nor do you give your attitude about the suit led.

First, consider the attempt to win the trick. Of course, there will be times when you want to capture the trick when you are in second position, but usually the pressure is not on you to do so for the simple reason that partner will be the last person to play to the trick.

Example. Dummy leads a low card of this suit in a no-trump contract.

8 7 5 2

(you)
K J 9 3

If partner has a high card in this suit he can play it at his turn. If partner has no high cards you are not favored to take any tricks as declarer can capture all of your cards. Playing high can never gain a trick for your side (in this suit), and it could certainly cost a trick if partner has a singleton honor.

Because of the possibility of such an occurrence the expression "second hand low" has been known to echo through the room in many bridge circles. Most of the do and don't cliches of card play are mechanical and have too many exceptions to be useful. This particular one is true relatively often. It refers specifically to the situation when the hand before you has led a low card.

Another example:

Q 6 4

(you)
A 8 5

K 10 9 2

J 7 3

Declarer leads the three from his hand. If you were to prematurely play your ace, declarer will eventually develop a trick with this suit. You should play low as partner is the last to play. Partner will capture the queen and later you will capture the jack, leaving declarer with no tricks in this suit.

It is certainly possible that there is some reason for you to win the trick in second position. For example, you may know that partner cannot possibly win it, or you may need to gain the lead at this point to lead another suit in order to beat the contract. Also, it is seldom correct to refuse to take the *setting* trick, regardless of what seat you are in. "Second hand low" is an expression people use to guide them to the play that will be right most of the time. It is only that. You will find that as you keep working at this game you will always need to be thinking. Bridge provides an excellent opportunity for developing and retaining an alert mind.

If you are in second position and the hand in front of you leads an honor, you have a very difficult situation. If you have a larger honor you should usually play it. Take a look at the following situations with dummy leading the queen:

a) Q 6 4	b) Q 6 4	c) Q 6 4
(you)	(you)	(you)
K 8 3	K 8 3	A 5 3
A 7 2	A J 2	K 8 7

In each case you must cover the queen or declarer will get an extra trick. The reason for covering is that partner may have secondary honors. In case a) partner has both the jack and 10 which are high after the queen, king, and ace are played. Of course, declarer shouldn't play the suit this way, but beginning players frequently do things like this. In case b), trick one of this suit would be queen-king-ace, and declarer has the jack which will provide a second trick. Notice if you allowed declarer's queen to win the trick he can now lead toward his jack and take *three* tricks. Case c): Again you must cover or you will allow declarer to win two tricks instead of one.

When one of touching honors is led, there is no need to cover the first one.

Q J 6 4

(you)
K 8 5 (or A 8 5)

With the queen led, play small. If the queen wins and now the jack is led you must cover as partner may have the ten. If dummy has touching honors, cover the last one played. You might ask, "What difference does it make if I covered the first one?" The answer is simply that it *may* cost, if for example partner had a singleton honor. The real point is that it never gains and you want to begin making plays that make sense. Card play should not be random.

There are very few exceptions to covering a (single) honor with an honor. The exceptions are fairly common sense but here is one worth looking at so one doesn't get caught asleep.

Declarer opened the bidding with one spade and dummy has:

Q 10 8 6 2

(you)
K 4

(declarer)

If declarer leads the queen from dummy play low. Even in the unlikely situation of partner having the jack, it would be singleton (remember, declarer opened one spade so he rates to have five). It cannot gain to cover and you'll have egg all over your face if partner has a singleton ace. It is a common ploy to go to dummy and lead the queen.

Even if the suit is as follows:

Q 10 8 6 2

K 4
A J 7 5 3

If you play small as declarer leads the queen, he may decide to play the ace hoping the king will drop—not the best percentage play, but people don't always know the best percentage plays. They don't need to if the defense is so friendly as to cover. This may seem like a lot of fuss over one trick, but one trick is often the difference between a contract making or breaking.

Try the following little quiz. Declarer opened one spade and dummy has.

Q 10 8 6 2

(you)
K 4

(declarer)

Declarer wins the opening lead of a different suit and returns a low spade to dummy. Do you play low or the king? This is another situation where defenders frequently go astray. If declarer had the ace, surely he would play it (or go to dummy for a finesse). You should play low, as partner almost certainly has the ace AND it is singleton.

FOURTH hand play will be given some coverage in the chapter on defensive signaling. Be aware of the fact that unless there is a very important reason to refuse the trick, the fourth hand should win the trick if it will otherwise be won by the opponents. Probably the clearest example of this is,

8 7 6 2

West　　　　　　　　　　　　　　　　　　East
A 5　　　　　　　　　　　　　　　　　　　K 4

Q J 10 9 3

Declarer leads low from dummy, East plays low, and declarer plays the nine from his hand. If West decides he doesn't want to "waste" his ace on the nine, he will later have the opportunity to capture his partner's king. Not a play which makes one look particularly spectacular.

VII
TRUMP MANAGEMENT

Effective handling of trump is a consideration on every hand that has a trump suit. Some hands present special problems and require a different technique from the norm.

Although, as mentioned previously, beginners tend to play every hand as a cross-ruff, there certainly is an occasion for this line of play. The following example illustrates a hand that must be played as a cross-ruff:

Hand #1

North
♠ K J 8 2
♥ 9
♦ A 9 7 5 2
♣ K 9 3

West
♠ 9 4 3
♥ J 4
♦ K J 10 6 4
♣ Q J 10

East
♠ 7 5
♥ A K 10 8 7
♦ Q 3
♣ 8 6 5 4

South
♠ A Q 10 6
♥ Q 6 5 3 2
♦ 8
♣ A 7 2

CONTRACT: 4 ♠
OPENING LEAD: ♣Q

Win the club king and lead a heart. Suppose the opponent on your right wins the king and returns a trump. Win in dummy and play the ace of diamonds and ruff a diamond. Now play the ace of clubs then ruff a heart small. When this wins, ruff a diamond, ruff a heart, ruff a diamond, ruff a heart. Notice these last four tricks cannot fail as by this point your trumps are high so couldn't be over-ruffed. The club ace must be cashed early, because as you are finishing the cross-ruff one opponent, may discard clubs. When you try to cash the ace, it may be ruffed. As a general technique in cross-ruff hands, the side suit winners must be cashed early.

There are many hands where pulling trump must be delayed for a few tricks for some specific purpose. In a cross-ruff hand, the objective is to take all of the trumps separately, so they are not pulled at all. If you try playing this hand by pulling trump, you will end up with only eight tricks. Had West happened to have led a trump on opening lead, and East continued a trump, when winning the heart, the hand would fail.

Hand #2

North
♠ A Q 2
♥ 9 7 5 3
♦ A K Q
♣ 7 5 3

West
♠ J 10 9
♥ Q 8 6 2
♦ J 9 8 7 3
♣ Q

East
♠ 8 5
♥ J 10
♦ 10 6
♣ A K J 10 9 4 2

South
♠ K 7 6 4 3
♥ A K 4
♦ 5 4 2
♣ 8 6

CONTRACT: 4 ♠
OPENING LEAD: ♣Q

The club lead is over-taken by East's king and he continues with the ace and the jack. What should you do?

If you ruff low, West over-ruffs, if you ruff with the king, you will have a trump loser. There is also a heart loser in this hand so the ship will sink. The solution is easy: discard your losing heart on the third club. This eliminates a loser that was inevitable and protects your trump holding. Dummy is now out of clubs also, so as the cards are, any further club leads will not harm you.

IF THE EAST-WEST TRUMPS WERE REVERSED, East could generate an effective defense. After the third club won the trick he could continue with a fourth club. West would trump with the eight, forcing declarer's queen and East would come to a natural trump trick. This defensive play is referred to as an uppercut. Although, it is usually bad defense to give declarer an opportunity to sluff a loser in one hand while trumping in the other, in this case East would have a purpose.

North
♠ J 10 3
♥ 8 6 2
♦ A Q 7 3
♣ Q J 5

West
♠ 8 7 5 4
♥ K 10 7 5 3
♦ J 8
♣ 10 4

East
♠ 9 6
♥ A Q J
♦ 10 9 6 5
♣ 9 8 7 6

South
♠ A K Q 2
♥ 9 4
♦ K 4 2
♣ A K 3 2

CONTRACT: 4 ♠
OPENING LEAD: ♥5

    Both you and your partner were reluctant to bid no trump without a heart stopper, so you settled on the 4-3 spade fit. The defense begins with a low heart which East wins with the ace and returns the queen followed by the jack. You have no loser to discard, but you must protect your trump holding. If you trump, you will be down to three trumps in each hand. Then, if the suit doesn't divide 3-3, you are out of luck. In this case you would be down two. Instead, you must discard a club or a diamond. Even if West overtakes the heart jack, any further leads of the suit could be handled by dummy.

Hand #4

North
- ♠ K Q 10
- ♥ A 9 5 4
- ♦ A K 3
- ♣ 4 3 2

West
- ♠ 8 7 5
- ♥ K Q 8 3 2
- ♦ 5 4 2
- ♣ J 7

East
- ♠ 9 6
- ♥ J 10 7
- ♦ 10 9 8 6
- ♣ 10 9 8 5

South
- ♠ A J 4 3 2
- ♥ 6
- ♦ Q J 7
- ♣ A K Q 6

CONTRACT: 7 ♠
OPENING LEAD: ♥K

If you pull trump and run your tricks, the contract will hinge on clubs being 3-3. There must be something better. If you know about squeezes, that would be a possibility, though not a very good one.

There is a fairly simple way to make this hand if the trumps are divided 3-2. As you already know, trumping in dummy usually extends your trumps. If you can trump ENOUGH times in your hand you can reverse this concept. If three hearts were trumped in your hand you will extend the trump tricks to six.

Win the heart ace and trump a heart low. Lead a trump to dummy's king followed by the trump queen. When both follow, you are in good shape. Trump another heart with the jack. Lead a diamond to dummy and trump the last heart with the ace. Your hand is now out of trump. Lead a diamond to dummy and pull the outstanding trump. This play is descriptively named the "dummy reversal."

Hand #5

North
♠ K Q 4
♥ 10 8 5 2
♦ 3
♣ A K 8 5 4

West
♠ 1095
♥ AKQ763
♦ —
♣ 10762

East
♠ 8763
♥ J94
♦ J964
♣ 93

South
♠ A J 2
♥ —
♦ A K Q 10 8 7 5 2
♣ Q J

CONTRACT: 7 ♦
OPENING LEAD: ♥K

You ruff the opening lead in your hand. Having no inkling as to the unfortunate trump break, you lay down the ace and get the bad news. You may want to play around with this hand as a double-dummy problem (meaning being able to look at all four hands). See if you can find a way to save your slam. As always, the opponents are not permitted an error. The solution lies in creating a situation where dummy is on lead with this position:

North

West

East
♠ —
♥ —
♦ J96
♣ —

South
♠ —
♥ —
♦ K Q 10
♣ —

.Recognizing this is the only legitimate way to make the contract, you must set out to create this position. It is necessary to reduce your trumps to the same number East has, which will mean trumping three more hearts, and still be able to get back to dummy. Dummy has four entries so the play has a chance.

Play a club to the ace and ruff a heart, then another club to dummy and ruff another heart. You will eventually need to play off all of your spades to create the position desired, so play the ace of spades then a spade to dummy. Ruff the fourth heart which completes your trump reduction. Now play your last spade to dummy and lead any card—East is trapped.

One of the problems in executing this play is planning the order to fit the hand pattern East has.

This line of play allows for East having a doubleton club. If the spade entries are used to ruff the two hearts, and a club entry to ruff the fourth heart, East will discard a club on the fourth heart which will cut off access to dummy. If East were to have three spades and three clubs, it would be necessary to do it the other way. Because you may have to figure out East's distribution in your planning, this play is considered to be an advanced play. It is called a "trump coup". It doesn't occur often, but when the need for this play arises and you successfully execute the coup, it is a good moment.

For a bit of reassurance, there is not always a choice of play as to the order of entries to the dummy. On the next hand, there are no choices to be made. The coup either works or it doesn't.

Hand #6

North
♠ A K Q
♥ 7 5 3
♦ 10 9 7 4 3 2
♣ 8

West
♠ J 9 8 6
♥ J 9 8 4
♦ A K 6 5
♣ 4

East
♠ 7 5 3
♥ 10 6 2
♦ Q J 8
♣ J 9 7 6

South
♠ 10 4 2
♥ A K Q
♦ —
♣ A K Q 10 5 3 2

CONTRACT: 7 ♣
OPENING LEAD: ♦ K

The first diamond is trumped in your hand and two high trumps are played, with West showing out on the second. East **must** have at least three spades and three hearts or there is no chance. Play off your three hearts and plan the trump reduction play. Play a spade, trump a diamond, another spade and another diamond ruff. Now a spade to the board and you have it.

VIII

TIMING AND ENTRIES

IT IS ESSENTIAL to develop the habit of planning ahead to make any kind of progress at this game. With some hands, critical decisions must be made early in the hand. This chapter is designed to reinforce this idea and provide additional exercise.

Hand #1

North
♠ 8 6 4 3
♥ 4 3 2
♦ A 5 4
♣ Q 6 2

South
♠ A K Q J 10 2
♥ A Q J
♦ K Q 3
♣ 4

CONTRACT: 6 ♠
OPENING LEAD: ♣A

The club ace is followed by a low club. This hand is not difficult, but a bit of carelessness (often caused by talking and playing at the same time) may lead to your ruin. Plan your play.

You will need a successful heart finesse to land this contract, and you will need two entries to dummy to take it twice. At trick two, the club queen is covered by East's king. You must ruff high as dummy has only the ace of diamonds for an entry. After pulling trump, your deuce will provide a very important second entry. This kind of play is routine for seasoned players simply because they have developed the habit of looking ahead.

On the next hand, South was overcome with the best hand he had ever seen and drove himself to slam.

Hand #2

North
♠ J 8 3 2
♥ 6 2
♦ 8 7 6 5 3
♣ Q J

South
♠ A K Q
♥ A K Q J 5 4
♦ A Q
♣ K 3

CONTRACT: 6 ♥
OPENING LEAD: ♣A

A hand like this makes a good story, especially when you can end it with "And I made it." Once again, dummy is pitiful. An entry is needed, and dummy has only one possible entry. Play the king of clubs under the ace. If West switches to another suit, you will pull trump, play off the top spades, go to dummy with a club and discard the diamond queen on the jack of spades. If West continues with a second club, the diamond finesse must be taken immediately.

Hand #3

North
- ♠ Q J 8
- ♥ 5 4
- ♦ 8 7 5
- ♣ A 8 5 4 2

West
- ♠ 9 7 6
- ♥ J 10 3
- ♦ A K Q 4 2
- ♣ 9 3

East
- ♠ 4
- ♥ K Q 9 8 7 2
- ♦ 6 3
- ♣ Q J 10 6

South
- ♠ A K 10 5 3 2
- ♥ A 6
- ♦ J 10 9
- ♣ K 7

THE AUCTION:

South	West	North	East
1S	Pass	2S	Pass
4S	Pass	Pass	Pass

OPENING LEAD: ♦ K

West begins by cashing his three top diamonds. East discards the nine of hearts on the third diamond, so West switches to the heart jack.

The club suit must be developed for a heart discard. A 3-3 break would make this hand easy, but you can also make it if clubs are 4-2 if you plan for it. You can play only one high trump from your hand as you must go after the club suit, keeping both the queen and the jack of trump for entries. Play the king of clubs followed by the ace and ruff a club with the ten. Next, play a low spade to the jack and ruff another club with the king. Pull the last trump with dummy's queen, and discard your heart on dummy's good club.

With the following hand, partner got a little carried away and put you in six spades.

Hand #4

North
♠ J 5 3
♥ 9 6 4
♦ A K Q
♣ A K 6 4

West
♠ 8 4
♥ K Q J 10 5
♦ J 8 2
♣ Q 5 2

East
♠ 10 9 6
♥ 8 2
♦ 10 9 7 6 5
♣ J 10 7

South
♠ A K Q 7 2
♥ A 7 3
♦ 4 3
♣ 9 8 3

CONTRACT: 6 ♠
OPENING LEAD: ♥K

One of your three losers could be discarded on the third diamond, but you would still be down one. Is there any hope for this contract?

The only chance is that clubs are 3-3 (as well as trumps and diamonds behaving). Play only two rounds of trumps from your hand as the jack must be preserved for an entry. Next, play three rounds of diamonds, pitching a club. Now play the ace and king of clubs and ruff a club. (A high ruff is best as it will prevent a possible down-two if the suit doesn't split 3-3). If clubs *are* 3-3, you are home. Play a trump to the jack, pulling the last trump and discard a losing heart on the thirteenth club.

With the following hand, you are in six diamonds. Cover the East-West hands and work out a plan to cope with the fact that you have one too many losers.

Hand #5

North
- ♠ A 6 5
- ♥ 5 4
- ♦ Q J 10
- ♣ 9 7 5 4 2

West
- ♠ 10 7 4
- ♥ Q J 9 7 3
- ♦ 5
- ♣ Q 10 6 3

East
- ♠ Q J 9 8
- ♥ K 10 6 2
- ♦ 9 4
- ♣ K J 8

South
- ♠ K 3 2
- ♥ A 8
- ♦ A K 8 7 6 3 2
- ♣ A

CONTRACT: 6 ♦
OPENING LEAD: ♥ Q

Dummy's club suit is pretty anemic, but the fact that there are five of them offers hope. If you could trump three of them, the last one might be good. You have six, so there are seven out. If they are divided 4-3 this will work if there are enough entries. You will need to get to dummy three times for ruffing and once more to be able to cash the last club. Dummy has three trump entries plus the ace of spades. Win the opening lead in your hand, play off the club ace and get going on setting up the thirteenth club.

It's fun to get good hands and even more fun when you get to a contract you can make. Try the next one.

Hand #6

North
- ♠ 5 3 2
- ♥ Q 10 5
- ♦ Q J 10 2
- ♣ 6 5 2

West
- ♠ J 8 7
- ♥ J 8 6
- ♦ 6 4 3
- ♣ J 8 7 4

East
- ♠ Q 10 9 6
- ♥ 9 7
- ♦ K 9 8 7 5
- ♣ Q 10

South
- ♠ A K 4
- ♥ A K 4 3 2
- ♦ A
- ♣ A K 9 3

THE AUCTION:

South	West	North	East
2C*	Pass	2D**	Pass
2H	Pass	3H***	Pass
6H	Pass	Pass	Pass

*	strong, artificial and forcing
**	negative
***	showing *some* values

OPENING LEAD: ♠7

You have a spade loser and at least one club loser. The diamond suit looks promising, but access to it is a problem.

After winning the spade, play the ace of diamonds followed by the ace of trumps. You need to get to dummy twice so your best shot is to lead low to dummy's 10 of hearts. If it wins, lead dummy's queen of diamonds. If East plays low, discard a loser, then lead the diamond jack. If East covers, ruff it and return to dummy with the trump queen. This play is called a ruffing finesse.

The next hand is an easy one of you give it some thought instead of pushing cards around.

Hand #7

North
- ♠ K Q 9
- ♥ 10 9
- ♦ 4 3 2
- ♣ J 10 7 5 4

West
- ♠ J 10 4 3 2
- ♥ J 4
- ♦ 9 6
- ♣ A K 3 2

East
- ♠ 8 7 6 5
- ♥ 8
- ♦ Q J 10 8
- ♣ Q 9 8 6

South
- ♠ A
- ♥ A K Q 7 6 5 3 2
- ♦ A K 7 5
- ♣ —

CONTRACT: 6 ♥
OPENING LEAD: ♣K

You actually have 13 tricks, but no way to cash them. If the diamonds split 3-3, you would have 12 tricks. You could improve upon that by playing all but one trump and the ace of spades (someone might discard a diamond from four if the suit were 4-2). However, this contract need not be left to chance. The slam is a near shoo-in if after winning the ace of spades, you lead a low heart towards dummy. You concede a needless trump trick to the jack, but now have a valuable entry to dummy. If West plays low, your nine wins, and if he plays the jack, you can get to dummy later with the ten of trump to discard your diamond losers on the high spades.

IX

PLAYING IN THE REAL WORLD

Sometimes the opponents are not in the auction. When they are, the information can be of value. There is a great deal of information available to you when you are declarer—what the opponents bid or didn't bid, what they led, and finally your analysis of winners and losers. Sometimes you have the tricks you need and don't really care whether or not the opponents bid or what they led. Other times, you will need the information. It's a good habit to be aware of everything happening at the table, so the information can be used when you need it. For example always pay attention to the **exact** card led. Absorb this, so later in the hand you don't begin to think "What was it she led?"

Hand #1

North
♠ 6 4
♥ Q 5 3
♦ A 10 3 2
♣ A 7 6 2

South
♠ A 8 3
♥ A K 4
♦ K J 5 4
♣ K 9 3

THE AUCTION:

South	West	North	East
1NT	Pass	3NT	Pass
Pass	Pass		

OPENING LEAD: ♠K

You have eight top winners available with a good diamond suit that easily could provide another trick. The opening lead is somewhat threatening. The king indicates a sequence, so the suit may be something such as KQJxx. It is good technique to hold off on taking your ace until the last possible moment in an attempt to break communication. This "hold-up" play is used mainly in no-trump contracts. After winning the ace it's time to tackle the diamond suit. You have a two way finesse, so if you were to lose to the queen, you have a choice as to which opponent would win it. Clearly, you don't want West to get the lead as presumably the long spade suit is in that hand. Play the king of diamonds and lead low to the ten. If East wins, he probably has no more spades. If he has exactly one more, the spade suit was 4-4 and you are safe.

With the next hand, you are in a three no-trump contract with the six of hearts led: East plays the ten and you win your queen.

Hand #2

North
- ♠ K Q 4
- ♥ 5 4
- ♦ 10 9 7 5
- ♣ A J 3 2

West
- ♠ 106
- ♥ A J 9 6 3 2
- ♦ 8 6 3
- ♣ 9 8

East
- ♠ 9 8 7 5
- ♥ 108
- ♦ K Q J 4
- ♣ Q 7 6

South
- ♠ A J 3 2
- ♥ K Q 7
- ♦ A 2
- ♣ K 10 5 4

THE AUCTION:

South	*West*	*North*	*East*
1NT	Pass	3NT	Pass
Pass	Pass		

OPENING LEAD: ♥6

You have seven top winners plus the heart trick. The club suit has at least one more trick available, which will be enough. With a little care in the play, this hand can not be defeated. Play a club to the ace, then low to the ten. Even if it loses, your contract is safe as you have the heart suit protected with West on lead. What you can't afford is for East to win a trick and lead through your heart king: the difference between making your contract and going down two.

With the two hands following, you are in 3NT. Notice the auction and plan your play.

Hand #3

North
- ♠ K 4 2
- ♥ K 2
- ♦ 10 8 4 2
- ♣ K J 7 5

South
- ♠ A Q 10
- ♥ J 7 4
- ♦ Q J
- ♣ A Q 8 6 3

THE AUCTION:

South	*West*	*North*	*East*
1NT	Pass	3NT	Pass
Pass	Pass		

OPENING LEAD: ♥ 5

Hand #4

North
- ♠ 9 7 3
- ♥ K 2
- ♦ K J 8 2
- ♣ A 7 6 3

South
- ♠ K 4
- ♥ J 7 4
- ♦ A Q 7 3
- ♣ K Q J 5

THE AUCTION:

South	*West*	*North*	*East*
1NT	2S	3NT	Pass
Pass	Pass		

OPENING LEAD: ♥ 5

With Hand #3, there are eight top tricks. Both the diamond and heart suits offer possible tricks. The heart suit is such that all you have to do is play low to ensure a trick. If RHO plays low, you win the trick, whereas if he plays either the ace or queen, you have two honors left and cannot be prevented from taking a trick. If you were to play the king and it lost to the ace, a heart back through your jack could set you if West started with, say, Q 10 8 5 3. Since no other suits are threatening, your contract is guaranteed by playing low from dummy at trick one.

With Hand #4 there is a different problem. West, who bid spades, made a creative lead in an attempt to get his partner on lead to lead a spade through declarer. If you play low in the heart suit, East has *two* chances to gain the lead and you can't afford a spade return from that hand. Your best bet is to try the heart king, hoping the ace is with West. If it is, you have nine tricks.

Hand #4 Complete

North
♠ 9 7 3
♥ K 2
♦ K J 8 2
♣ A 7 6 3

West
♠ A Q J 8 5
♥ A 6 5
♦ 6 4
♣ 10 8 4

East
♠ 10 6 2
♥ Q 10 9 8 3
♦ 10 9 5
♣ 9 2

South
♠ K 4
♥ J 7 4
♦ A Q 7 3
♣ K Q J 5

With the following hand, notice the auction. West leads the king of diamonds and continues with the ace. East follows small to the first trick and discards the king of hearts on the second. West cashes the diamond queen and with such a clear signal from partner, switches to a heart.

Hand #5

North
♠ Q J 10 2
♥ 8 2
♦ 7 4 3 2
♣ A Q J

South
♠ A K 9 7 5 4 3
♥ A 3
♦ J 10 5
♣ 8

THE AUCTION:

West	North	East	South
	Pass	Pass	1S
Pass	3S	Pass	4S
Pass	Pass	Pass	

With three diamonds having been cashed, you are booked and have a heart loser with which to contend. After winning the heart ace, and pulling trump, you must tackle the club suit. If West has the king, a straight finesse would work, as you could discard your losing heart on the club ace. If East has the club king you could take a ruffing finesse through him by playing the ace, then leading the queen. If East plays low, you discard the losing heart. If he covers, ruff it and your club jack is now established for a heart discard. (You have an entry in the trump suit).

Which is more likely to work? Clearly the ruffing finesse is right. If you look back at the auction, West is known to have started with AKQxx of diamonds. If he also had the club king, surely he would have overcalled.

North
♠ A 10 3
♥ 6 5 3
♦ K Q J
♣ K Q 4 3

West
♠ Q 9 8 6 5 2
♥ 4
♦ 7 6 5
♣ A 6 2

East
♠ 7
♥ Q J 10 9 8 7 2
♦ 10 8 4
♣ 8 7

South
♠ K J 4
♥ A K
♦ A 9 3 2
♣ J 10 9 5

THE AUCTION:

West	North	East	South
		3H	3NT
Pass	6NT	Pass	Pass
Pass			

OPENING LEAD: ♥4

You have eight top winners, three more which will be coming to you in the club suit and there is a two-way finesse available in the spade suit. After winning the opening lead, drive out the ace of clubs. West wins and plays another club. On the third round, East discards a heart. You now play three rounds of diamonds as all follow. As you cash your last two minor suit cards, East discards two hearts and West two spades. How do you play the spade suit?

What many would do in this case, is notice that the three heart bidder had only QJ10xxxx of hearts and no other high cards, leaving the thought that he probably has the queen of spades. In addition to that, LHO discarded two spades. This kind of thinking is certainly better than guessing, but sometimes there is more specific information available. You may think that counting out complete hands is something only experts do. Experts started somewhere. An easy starting place is when you are declarer and an opponent has made a preemptive bid. East is presumed to have started out with seven hearts, which leaves only six other cards in his hand. He has followed to two rounds of clubs and **three** rounds of diamonds. This leaves only one spade in his hand. Although it is valid to presume he started out with seven hearts, you can actually know for sure by playing your other heart honor (West should show out). Now play the king of spades and a low spade to the ten for a "marked" finesse.

North
♠ 8 6 4
♥ 7 6 4 3
♦ K J 4
♣ A J 6

West
♠ A K 10 7 2
♥ A Q J 10
♦ 8 5 2
♣ 4

East
♠ 9 5
♥ 9 8 2
♦ 7 6
♣ Q 8 7 5 3 2

South
♠ Q J 3
♥ K 5
♦ A Q 10 9 3
♣ K 10 9

THE AUCTION:

South	West	North	East
	1S	Pass	Pass
2D	2H	3D	Pass
3NT	Pass	Pass	Pass

OPENING LEAD: ♠7

The spade lead is won in your hand, which gives you eight tricks. You now run the five diamonds as West follows to three rounds, then discards two hearts and East discards a spade and two clubs. The club position is now transparent. West bid spades and hearts so must have at least nine of them plus he followed to three diamonds. He can have no more than one club. Play a club to the ace and take the marked finesse.

Sometimes there may be no information available from the bidding, but the play reveals the distribution.

Hand #8

North
♠ A K Q
♥ A 10 6
♦ A Q 4
♣ 6 5 3 2

South
♠ J 8 7
♥ K J 4
♦ K J 10 8 6
♣ A K

CONTRACT: 7NT
OPENING LEAD: ♣Q

After you opened 1NT, partner bid 5NT (inviting seven). With 16 HCP, and a good five card suit you accepted. Opponents are seldom in the auction when you hold cards like this. Unfortunately, you will have to guess the heart suit to make this, unless you can get some information about the opponents cards. As you play the diamonds West follows to three rounds then discards two small spades. East parts with two clubs and a spade. As you play the three top spades, West discards a club and East a heart. When you play the other high club, West follows and East discards another heart. Figure out what you know about the distribution of the opponent's cards.

At this point you have a complete count of the hand. West started out with exactly four clubs as East played three, then showed out. West also produced exactly four spades and followed to three rounds of diamonds. The heart suit was therefore two in West's hand and five in East's. The heart queen therefore, has a much greater likelihood (5:2) of being in the East hand. Play a heart to the ace and finesse the jack.

Hand #9

North
- ♠ Q 7 6 2
- ♥ 10 8 6 4 2
- ♦ A J 9
- ♣ K

West
- ♠ J 10 9 3
- ♥ —
- ♦ 10 7 6 4
- ♣ A 9 6 3 2

East
- ♠ A K 8 4
- ♥ A 9
- ♦ Q 8 5
- ♣ Q J 10 8

South
- ♠ 5
- ♥ K Q J 7 5 3
- ♦ K 3 2
- ♣ 7 5 4

THE AUCTION:

West	North	East	South
		1NT	2H
Pass	4H	Pass	Pass
Pass			

OPENING LEAD: ♠J

Either someone forgot to tell partner about invitational bids, or he is very impressed with your dummy play. You have four possible losers. The jack of spades holds the first trick and a spade is continued which you ruff. The king of trump is played which East wins as West discards the club six. You ruff the spade return and pull the remaining trump. When you lead a club to the king, West wins and returns another spade. At this point the diamond finesse looks dismal. You and dummy have a combined 19 HCP and West had the ace of clubs and jack of spades. East must have the diamond queen, since he wouldn't open 1NT with only 14 HCP. The diamond queen isn't likely to be doubleton as East is known to have a doubleton heart. Is the contract hopeless or can you come up with a plan?

Ruff a club in dummy and lead the diamond jack. If East doesn't cover, the jack would win, but chances are he will play the queen. If so, win the king and lead another diamond towards the nine to finesse against West's ten. This play is referred to as a backward finesse, but might be more accurately described as a transfer finesse. It's not a play one uses often as it requires **two** cards to be in a certain place which is only half as likely to work as a straight finesse. In this case, however, the straight finesse was certain to lose, so this play was necessary.

X

DEFENSIVE SIGNALING

During the defense of a hand, there are three distinctly different pieces of information that can be passed across the table that will inform partner about some important feature of your hand.

ATTITUDE refers to playing a particular card, high or low, and suggesting that you have or don't have interest in that suit.

COUNT refers to the situation when you tell partner whether you have an even or odd number of cards in a particular suit.

SUIT PREFERENCE refers to that somewhat less common situation of playing a particular card of one suit to give information about another.

Each of these three methods of communication can provide valuable information to partner. This information will be communicated only if both you and partner know under what conditions each piece of information is being transmitted. For example, it will be somewhat ineffective if you attempt to show partner that you have an important card in a particular suit (attitude), if he thinks you are telling how many cards you have— or if you think you are telling how many cards you have, and he thinks you are telling something about another suit, etc. Unless both people take the trouble to become clear about this, no information at all is transmitted.

For people who play a very casual game of bridge, it would make sense to get a good understanding about **attitude** and worry about the other two things later. This is because attitude signals occur frequently and give information that is easy to understand. However, as you become excited about this game, you will want to pass and receive as much information as possible so you don't have to guess at what to do to defeat a contract: You will **know**. After you understand the following information, find your favorite partner and have him read this. If he refuses, beg, threaten, or find a new partner.

ATTITUDE—There was some discussion of this in the chapter on third hand play, but to recap, there are two situations when the bridge players of the world show their attitude or interest in a particular suit. The first is when your side leads a high card or when your side leads any card and the opponent next to play wins it. You can let partner know if you have interest in his continuing this suit by playing the highest card you can afford.

Example:

Dummy
A 6 2

Partner leads
♥ 4

You have
K 8 5

If declarer plays dummys ace, you play the *eight*, in an attempt to let partner know you would like this suit continued as you have an important card. This type of signal is very well known. Most people learn this fairly early in their bridge career.

The other situation is when you have no more cards in the suit led and are about to make a discard. If you discard a high card of another suit, it implies you have something important in that suit and would like for partner to lead it when he obtains the lead. Conversely, a low card indicates **lack** of interest in the suit which you discarded. Occasionally there is a question as to whether the card played was high or low. Although a discard of six or higher is frequently intended to encourage, it is important to notice the other spot cards visable, i.e., partner discards a six, and between your hand and dummy you can see the 5, 4, 3, and 2 of the suit, partner clearly is playing the lowest card he has. Because of this, if you want to signal strength in a certain suit, play the highest card you can afford.

Sometimes, you can't afford a high card of a suit you want led, e.g. you hold the A K Q, so the best you can do is discard a low card of a suit you **don't** want led. Also, sometimes you may wish for partner to shift to a suit in which you hold A K 3 2. If you have the opportunity to make two discards, you can play the three followed by the two—not a very dramatic "come on", but it is the best you can do. If partner is watching your cards, he will notice your high-low signal. Anemic though it may seem, it will get the message across.

As was mentioned earlier, attitude signals are easy and get information across. As you start adding other signals, be sure to keep track of when attitude applies as it is the most important.

COUNT—The number of cards you have in a particular suit can be shown by playing "up the line" from odd numbers and "high-low" from even numbers. The times when it makes sense to give your count is when DECLARER leads a suit. As a rule, he will be playing a suit that offers hope of developing winners for the offense. As a defender, it makes little sense to give your attitude about this suit. If the cards are not placed where he had hoped, your side will be in a good position. Since attitude doesn't apply in this situation, you and partner can use this opportunity to exchange information as to how many cards you hold in the suit. Sometimes this information can be very valuable.

Hand #1

North
- ♠ K Q J 10
- ♥ 7 6 3 2
- ♦ 9 8 7 5
- ♣ A

West
- ♠ 9 6 2
- ♥ Q 4
- ♦ 4 3 2
- ♣ Q 10 5 4 2

East *(you)*
- ♠ A 8 4 3
- ♥ K J 10 5
- ♦ J 6
- ♣ J 7 6

South
- ♠ 7 5
- ♥ A 9 8
- ♦ A K Q 10
- ♣ K 9 8 3

THE AUCTION:

South	*West*	*North*	*East*
1NT	Pass	2C	Pass
2D	Pass	3NT	Pass
Pass	Pass		

OPENING LEAD: ♣4

Partner's lead removes a valuable entry to dummy. At trick two, declarer leads the king of spades which you refuse in an attempt to cut declarer off from dummy. If declarer has three spades, you should take the third one. If he has two, you should take the second one as he can never get back to his remaining winner or winners. The answer should come from partner. He will play the two (going up the line) which shows an odd number. Partner can't have five as declarer opened one no trump, and if partner has only **one** it doesn't matter what you do. The relevant holdings are two and three. Partner is showing an odd number so if he has three, declarer would have two. Notice with this hand it is imperative for you to take specifically the *second* round to prevent declarer from taking nine tricks.

The above situation can occur in a suit contract as well. The contract is four spades with the king of diamonds led:

Hand #2

North
♠ 4 3 2
♥ 8 7 2
♦ 9 6 4
♣ K Q J 6

West
♠ 7 6 5
♥ 10 6 5 3
♦ A K 3
♣ 10 5 3

East *(you)*
♠ 10 8
♥ K Q J 9
♦ 8 7 5 2
♣ A 7 2

South
♠ A K Q J 9
♥ A 4
♦ Q J 10
♣ 9 8 4

Although you play a low diamond at trick one, partner elects to continue with the ace and a third diamond, which declarer wins. Declarer pulls trumps in three rounds and leads a club to the jack as partner plays the three. Partner is showing an odd number, as you have the two. If partner has three clubs, declarer also has three. If the suit is splitting 3-3, it is imperative to hold up on the club ace until the third round. Declarer will have a winning club on the board on which he could discard a losing heart, but will have no way to get to it.

Now suppose partner's odd number of clubs is five, so declarer has a singleton. Look at the rest of declarer's hand. He is known to have five trump and exactly three diamonds. If he has only one club, he has four hearts so you can easily win two or three heart tricks to defeat the contract. There is no risk in refusing the first club, but there is a great risk in taking it.

Because of the fact that it will enable partner to "count out" a hand by showing count, many partnerships fairly routinely give count when they are following to the suit declarer is leading. Yes, this information is available to declarer as well, but frequently doesn't help him, as in the first two examples. Also, many declarers you will play against do not know how, or have not developed the habit of counting a hand. If you do, you will have a tremendous advantage. As you may suspect, this takes some concentration. It doesn't work well if you try to carry on a conversation at the same time.

SUIT PREFERENCE—Suit preference signals are used when the situation is such that neither attitude nor count is of importance. There are two situations which are regarded as standard suit preference: 1) When a defender plays a card that his partner may trump and will need to know what to lead back, and 2) In a suit contract when dummy has a singleton of the suit led.

Hand #3

North
♠ Q J 4
♥ 10 6 5 2
♦ 9 5 4 3
♣ K Q

West
♠ 10 9 3 2
♥ 4
♦ J 8 6 2
♣ J 8 6 4

East
♠ 6
♥ A 9 8 7 3
♦ 10 7
♣ A 10 7 5 2

South
♠ A K 8 7 5
♥ K Q J
♦ A K Q
♣ 9 3

THE AUCTION:

South	*West*	*North*	*East*
1S	Pass	2S	Pass
4S	Pass	Pass	Pass

You lead your singleton heart and partner wins the ace and returns a heart for you to ruff. If you can get partner on lead again, you will defeat this contract. How do you know which minor suit to try? The answer should come from partner. If he suspected you were going to trump this trick he should tell you in what suit he can next win the lead. If he returns the heart three (his lowest) he is asking for a club (the lower of the side suits) return. If he plays the heart nine, he is asking for a diamond (the higher of the side suits) return. If he has no preference, he returns a middle card. Notice that there are always two remaining suits, as one is being trumped and one is the trump suit. If a person has a quick entry in the trump suit usually no signal is needed as the lead easily can be obtained. In the example hand, partner returns the heart three which you trump. When you return a club, partner wins and leads another heart to defeat the contract.

Another common situation for suit preference is the following:

Hand #4

North
♠ Q J 8 4
♥ 6
♦ K 6 3 2
♣ K J 3 2

West
♠ K 7
♥ K Q J 8 2
♦ J 10 8
♣ 10 9 8

East
♠ 5 2
♥ 9 7 5 4 3
♦ A Q 9
♣ 7 6 5

South
♠ A 10 9 6 3
♥ A 10
♦ 7 5 4
♣ A Q 4

CONTRACT: 4 ♠

Partner leads the heart king. It is seldom that you would want partner to continue a suit that declarer can ruff in dummy. Therefore, when partner leads a suit in which dummy has a singleton, it is fairly standard practice to indicate which other suit is of interest to you. In this case, the two remaining suits are diamonds and clubs. Since you have important values in diamonds, play the nine of hearts. Again, your lowest heart would suggest interest in clubs and a middle one would show indifference. Partner will note your play of the nine so when he gains the lead with the trump king, he will return the jack of diamonds which will set the contract, since you will take three diamond tricks plus the trump king. Notice if he returned anything else declarer would win, pull the last trump, play off the top clubs, and discard a diamond on the long club. A difference between the contract making or being set.

It should be pointed out that when making a play which gives important information, it is unethical to call attention to it. Giving partner a meaningful look at the point you play the card, is highly improper.

IN REVIEW, show attitude towards a suit when your side leads it or when making a discard; show count when following to a suit declarer is leading; and use a suit preference signal when partner may be trumping the card you lead or when dummy has a singleton. Experienced partnerships may find situations in which there are exceptions. However, it is best to become secure in the usual applications before worrying about possible exceptions.

Showing count in the trump suit is different from other suits. A high-low signal in the trump suit, such as playing the five followed by the two shows an *odd* number (three or five). It is referred to as a TRUMP ECHO and often indicates a desire to trump something.

It may be of value to point out that defense is more than a mechanical exchange of information. SIGNALING SHOULD BE AN AID. It is not intended to replace thinking.

XI

PLAYING IT SAFE

Sometimes in the play of a hand, there is a suit combination which, if played carefully, will produce the tricks needed even though there is a bad break. This type of careful play is referred to in bridge circles as a "safety play." The simplest example of this is a suit such as:

a). A 10 5 4
   K Q 9 3 2

The only possible problem is a 4-0 break. By playing the king or queen first, you will discover the bad break and since you have both the ten and nine, you can finesse in either direction. In a broad sense, this is a "safety play." Note that if you were to cash the ace first, you would lose a trick if West held all four cards.

Most often the term is used to describe a situation when you are willing to sacrifice an over-trick to increase your chances of taking a specific number of tricks. In this example you need five tricks:

b). A 9 2
   K 10 7 6 5 4

You have nine cards, so if you were to play the ace and king and the suit broke 2-2, you would lose no tricks. With a 3-1 break, you would probably lose one trick. (The reason you wouldn't necessarily have a loser is because if you played one of your high honors and the queen or jack fell, you might be in a position to finesse against the other honor).

Suppose, however, this is your trump suit and you are in a small slam. You have no outside losers, so the only ugly thing that can happen to you is a 4-0 break. If you were to play the ace first, you would lose two tricks with QJxx on your left, or if you were to play the king first you would lose two tricks with QJxx on your right. You can guard against either holding by leading low from your hand towards the nine, or low from dummy towards the 10. Suppose you won the first trick in your hand. Play a low trump towards the nine; if LHO plays low, play the nine. If it loses to the jack or queen, you did not get a 4-0 break so the remaining cards will be picked up with your ace and king. If LHO has Q J 8 3 and plays small, your nine will win. If he plays the jack (not his best play) you will win the ace and he will score only the queen. If LHO shows out as you play from your hand at trick two, it will be easy. Simply win the ace and lead towards the king-ten. Again, the opponents can take only one trick.

This line of play is a safety play as it guards against a bad break. Given that no side suit is about to be trumped, you will **never** lose more than one trump trick with this play. It will cost you an overtrick, however, if the suit is divided 2-2. When facing the conditions described above, the overtrick is of little importance. You want to make the slam!

Safety plays are vitally important for those who play rubber bridge. Understanding them is also important in duplicate bridge, even though over-tricks are important. First, it will heighten your awareness of what can happen in a given suit. Secondly, there are times that your contract is so good that you should go all out to make it. Thirdly, a part of duplicate tournaments involves team play, where emphasis is on making the contract rather than being concerned about over-tricks. To sum it up, studying safety plays will improve your card play.

The following examples are safety plays in the broad sense as in example a. These are not so much safety plays as correct plays.

1.	2.	3.	4.	5.
A 9 3	A 6 4	A Q 10 6 5	K 10 3 2	K Q 9 6 5
K Q 10 6 5 4	K 10 5 3 2	K 4 3	A Q 6 5	A 8 4 2
Six tricks	Four tricks	Five tricks	Four tricks	Five tricks

1. Play the king or queen. If you discover that the suit splits 4-0, you can finesse in either direction—100% for no losers.
2. Play the ace, and if both follow small, play low towards your hand. If RHO plays low, insert the ten. This play costs nothing as you have to lose a trick in any case and will guard against QJxx on your right.
3. Play a high honor from the upper hand followed by the king. You will now know if there is a 4-1 break. You will finesse if there are four to the jack on the left (the only 4-1 break you can handle).
4. Play the ace and queen. Again you will finesse if there proves to be jack-fourth on your left.
5. Play the ace. This may look deceptively similar to #3, but it's not. The only 4-0 break you can guard against is J10xx on the left. By leading towards the KQ9 twice, you can pick up the whole suit. If the bad split should exist you will know it when you play the ace.

The next examples are safety plays in the more typical usage of the term in that the purpose is not to find the best play for the greatest amount of tricks, but rather the best play for the REQUIRED amount of tricks.

6.	7.	8.	9.	10.
K965	8765	J53	AJ32	AKQ64
A10432	AQ1042	AK942	K76	32
Four tricks	Four tricks	Four tricks	Three tricks	Four tricks, no outside entry to dummy

6. Play low from either hand planning to play the ten or nine if an opponent plays small. If it loses, you did not get a 4-0 break, which is the only way you would lose two tricks. This play may cost an over-trick, but insures no more than one loser.

7. Play the ace, then go to dummy to lead low towards the queen-ten, covering any card by East. The problem with leading towards the queen for a first round finesse, is that if it loses you don't know whether to play for an original:

K/Jxx   or   KJ/xx

If KJx or KJxx are off side, no play will work, but if one of the two listed above is the case, playing the ace first eliminates the guess.

8. Play the ace, then lead towards the jack. This will hold the losers to one trick if LHO started with Q10xx, and if he shows out on the second round, you will play the jack which will lose to the queen. Later you will get back to the upper hand to lead towards the king-nine for a finesse against the ten. Notice that the nine can be an important card. This play will guard against **any** 4-1 break. If, instead of the nine, you had lower card, this play is still correct as it will hold you to one loser with any four cards on your left. If your hopes were to lose *no* tricks, your best bet would be to play the ace and king hoping for the doubleton queen to fall. The play of the ace followed by a low card is the safest play to win **four** tricks.

9. If you needed to take four tricks with this suit you would play the king, then finesse the jack, hoping that the queen is on side and the suit breaks 3-3. This is not the best or safest way to get **three** tricks. Play the ace and king, then lead up to the jack. You will take three tricks always when the queen is on the left, anytime there is a 3-3 break, AND with the doubleton queen on your right.

10. If you were to play the ace, king, and queen of this suit and it broke
    3-3 you would win five tricks. If, however, the split were 4-2, you would
    win only three tricks with this play, as there are no entries to dummy.
    Your best play for four tricks is to lose the first round by playing low
    from both hands. Now you will win four tricks with any 3-3 or 4-2 break.

If you review the above examples periodically, you will find that you will
spot them, even variations of them, when they come up in a hand.

With the following hand, you are in six spades, vulnerable, playing against
someone who has been getting on your nerves all evening. With careful play
this contact is a near certainty:

Hand #1

North
- ♠ A 10 4
- ♥ 7 2
- ♦ A 8 7 4
- ♣ A 9 6 4

West
- ♠ Q J 7 6
- ♥ J 10 9 4
- ♦ 9 5
- ♣ Q 10 5

East
- ♠ —
- ♥ 8 6 5 3
- ♦ Q J 6 3 2
- ♣ J 7 3 2

South
- ♠ K 9 8 5 3 2
- ♥ A K Q
- ♦ K 10
- ♣ K 8

OPENING LEAD: ♥ J

After winning the heart in hand, lead a low spade to the ten. This will
guard against any 4-0 trump break and the chance of anything getting ruffed
is extremely slim. Notice that this hand is based on example #6.

Hand #2

North
- ♠ K 6 4
- ♥ 8 7 4
- ♦ A Q 7 3
- ♣ 9 6 2

West
- ♠ 9
- ♥ K 10 9 5
- ♦ K 6 5 2
- ♣ Q 7 5 4

East
- ♠ Q J 8 7
- ♥ Q J 3 2
- ♦ J 10 9
- ♣ J 8

South
- ♠ A 10 5 3 2
- ♥ A 6
- ♦ 8 4
- ♣ A K 10 3

THE AUCTION:

South	*West*	*North*	*East*
1S	Pass	2S	Pass
3S	Pass	4S	Pass
Pass	Pass		

OPENING LEAD: ♦2

The diamond finesse is a must as there is most likely a loser in each of the other suits. When the queen holds, play the king of trump. When both follow small, lead a low trump towards your hand and if RHO plays small, play the ten. It can't cost, as you have a certain loser anyway and as the cards are, it will save a trick.

Hand #3

North
- ♠ 7 6 3
- ♥ 7 5 2
- ♦ A K Q 4 3
- ♣ 6 4

West
- ♠ K J 8 5 4
- ♥ 10 9
- ♦ 8 5
- ♣ K 10 9 7

East
- ♠ 10 9
- ♥ Q J 8 3
- ♦ J 10 9 7
- ♣ Q J 3

South
- ♠ A Q 2
- ♥ A K 6 4
- ♦ 6 2
- ♣ A 8 5 2

THE AUCTION:

South	West	North	East
		Pass	Pass
1NT	Pass	3NT	Pass
Pass	Pass		

OPENING LEAD: ♠5

Because a spade is led, you have eight top tricks. All you need is one extra diamond trick. Since dummy has no outside entries, play a low diamond from both hands at trick two so you can cope with a 4-2 break.

Hand #4

North
- ♠ 6 5 3
- ♥ A J 3 2
- ♦ 6 4
- ♣ K 10 4 3

West
- ♠ Q 10 8 4
- ♥ 10 8 6 5
- ♦ A
- ♣ J 9 7 5

East
- ♠ J 9 7 2
- ♥ Q 9
- ♦ K Q 8 7 5 3
- ♣ 8

South
- ♠ A K
- ♥ K 7 4
- ♦ J 10 9 2
- ♣ A Q 6 2

THE AUCTION:

South	West	North	East
1NT	Pass	2C	Pass
2D	Pass	2NT	Pass
3NT	Pass	Pass	Pass

OPENING LEAD: ♠4

There are seven top winners with both red suits looking promising. Play the ace and queen of clubs to test that suit. When RHO shows out, take the marked finesse which puts you up to eight tricks. Leave the king of clubs in dummy as you may need it for an entry. Since you need to develop only one more trick and can afford to lose the lead, take the safety play in hearts; play the ace, then king. You will be rewarded when the queen drops doubleton off-side.

Hand #5

North
♠ K Q
♥ J 6 3
♦ Q J 4
♣ A 8 5 3 2

West
♠ J 10 9 2
♥ Q 10 8 4
♦ 9 5
♣ 10 7 4

East
♠ 8 7 6 3
♥ 9
♦ 10 8 6 2
♣ K Q J 6

South
♠ A 5 4
♥ A K 7 5 2
♦ A K 7 3
♣ 9

THE AUCTION:

South	West	North	East
1H	Pass	2C	Pass
2D	Pass	4H	Pass
6H	Pass	Pass	Pass

OPENING LEAD: ♠J

Since you have no losers outside of the trump suit, take the best play to hold your trump losers to one. Win the queen of spades and play a low heart to the ace followed by low to the jack, guarding against queen-fourth on the left.

Hand #6

North
- ♠ A J
- ♥ 8 7 6 4
- ♦ Q 3 2
- ♣ Q 8 6 4

West
- ♠ 9 8 6 4
- ♥ K
- ♦ J 8 6 5
- ♣ J 10 9 3

East
- ♠ 10 7 5
- ♥ J 9 2
- ♦ 10 9 7
- ♣ K 7 5 2

South
- ♠ K Q 3 2
- ♥ A Q 10 5 3
- ♦ A K 4
- ♣ A

CONTRACT: 6 ♥
OPENING LEAD: ♣J

After winning the club ace, lay down the ace of hearts intending to get to dummy to lead towards the queen. However, when the king falls, your troubles are over. The problem many people would have with this hand is that they would play a spade to the jack to finesse the queen of hearts. When it loses they have to guess whether the jack will now fall under the ace, or if they should finesse again. If they guess wrong, they are down. Also, if one were to lead low to the ten of hearts and it lost to the jack there would be guess. Playing the ace first eliminates the guess.

The next hand is also a type of safety play.

Hand #7

North
♠ K 5 3 2
♥ 8 5 4
♦ Q J 9 3
♣ A K

South
♠ A J 7 6
♥ 10 9
♦ A K 7 6
♣ Q 5 3

CONTRACT: 4 ♠
OPENING LEAD: ♦ 2

The best play for no losers in the spade suit is of course to play the king and finesse the jack. With this hand, you are afraid of a diamond ruff if you lose the finesse, so you play the two top spades. This play in the trump suit protects against a bad split in a side suit, and with the diamond lead, you've been warned of a bad split.

XII

PLAYING WITH YOUR OPPONENTS HELP

There are numerous situations in bridge where you need to enlist the help of your opponents in making a contract. With the following suit combinations you are attempting to get the number of tricks listed:

1.	2.	3.	4.
J54	KJ2	K2	A92
Q32	A104	J74	K105
One trick	Three tricks	One trick	Three tricks

1. If a friendly opponent were to lead this suit, you are guaranteed a trick simply by playing a low card from whichever hand plays second.
2. Left to your own devices, you will finesse one way or another and lose about half the time. You may be able to improve upon the odds somewhat by being aware of the bidding and what distribution you have observed in the other suits. Nevertheless, you have a guess to make. If a friendly opponent leads the suit your problem is eliminated.
3. If you have to attack this suit yourself, the king could lose to the ace and the jack to the queen. If either opponent leads it, you have a trick.
4. Left to your own devices your chances of three tricks are exceedingly slim. It would take either the queen-jack doubleton or a singleton honor in one hand and taking a finesse through the other. If either opponent leads the suit your chances go way up.

```
          a)  A92                    b)  A92
  J843               Q76     QJ74               863
          K105                       K105
```

Case a. You could come to three tricks with either opponent on lead. If West leads the three, play the two from dummy and capture East's queen with your king. Then finesse against West's jack.

Case b. If West were on lead, obviously he can't lead low as your ten would win. If he leads the queen, you will win the king and have the same position as in the first example.

This suit combination provides an opportunity for an alert defender to shine. Look at case a. If East were on lead, instead of making the normal lead of low from an honor, he could make a deceptive lead of the queen. Although you could win the king and finesse against West's jack, you would think the jack was on your right, so would win the ace in dummy and finesse towards your king-ten.

Since even an experienced card player may be caught napping in a situation like this, as well as the fact that he may have been dealt both honors, it's usually in your best interest to assume his carding is honest. When players first start learning about false carding they sometimes develop a paranoia—thinking people are always trying to fool them. Actually, most of the time it's in the best interest of defenders to be as descriptive as possible in their card play—and they usually attempt to do so.

So, it has been established that with some suit combinations the opponents can work for your side. There is still the question of how you talk them into it.

Hand #1

North
- ♠ A 8 2
- ♥ A 10 3 2
- ♦ J 8 4
- ♣ A 6 3

West
- ♠ 10 5 3
- ♥ J 9 8
- ♦ A 7 6
- ♣ Q J 9 7

East
- ♠ Q J 9 6
- ♥ 6
- ♦ K 10 9 5
- ♣ 10 8 5 2

South
- ♠ K 7 4
- ♥ K Q 7 5 4
- ♦ Q 3 2
- ♣ K 4

CONTRACT: 4 ♥
OPENING LEAD: ♣Q

You have a spade loser and likely three diamond losers. After winning the club king, play the king, queen and ace of trumps. Next, play the ace of clubs and trump a club in your hand coming down to this position:

♠ A 8 2
♥ 10
♦ J 8 4
♣ —

♠ K 7 4
♥ 7
♦ Q 3 2
♣ —

Since the spade loser is inevitable, play your two top spades and give up the third round. Because both clubs and spades have been eliminated from your hand, the opponent who wins has no happy choice. Either he will have to break the diamond suit or lead a club or a spade, which would allow you to trump in one hand and discard a diamond loser from the other. The process of creating this set up is referred to as "stripping the hand." The play itself is called a THROW-IN or more commonly an END PLAY because typically it occurs towards the end of a hand.

Hand #2

North
♠ Q 10 9 5 4
♥ A Q 5
♦ Q J
♣ K J 2

South
♠ A K 8 3 2
♥ K 9 8
♦ A 4
♣ A 10 4

CONTRACT: 6 ♠
OPENING LEAD: ♥ J

You win the heart lead with dummy's queen. What are your chances of making this contract? Most people would pull trump and finesse the diamond. If that loses, later they would try to guess which way to finesse the club. That has about a 75 percent chance of success. Can you improve on those odds?

You were handed a bone by having both the queen and jack of diamonds. It seems wasteful not to attempt to develop a second trick in the diamond suit. However, you can guarantee your contract by pulling trump, playing the other two winning hearts, then playing the ace and another diamond. Whoever wins either will have to break clubs, eliminating the guess, or return a red suit which would give you a sluff and a ruff, again eliminating your possible club loser. You increased your odds from 75 percent to 100 percent. Notice the hand must be stripped so that the opponent who wins has no safe exit card. If, for example, the two heart winners had not been cashed, the play wouldn't work.

Hand #3

North
- ♠ 8 5 2
- ♥ 8 3 2
- ♦ A 9 2
- ♣ K J 7 5

West
- ♠ Q J 3
- ♥ J 10 9
- ♦ J 8 5 3
- ♣ 10 6 3

East
- ♠ 10 9 7 6
- ♥ 7 6 5 4
- ♦ Q 7 6
- ♣ 9 8

South
- ♠ A K 4
- ♥ A K Q
- ♦ K 10 4
- ♣ A Q 4 2

CONTRACT: 6NT
OPENING LEAD: ♥ J

You have enough points for the slam but can count only 11 tricks. After winning the heart, run your four club winners. LHO discards a diamond and RHO discards two hearts (clubs were 3-2). As you play two more rounds of hearts you discover they were 4-3 as LHO follows and RHO, who had sluffed two of them, now discards a low spade on your last heart. This end play isn't iron-clad like the last two, but the best bet at this point is to play the ace, king and another spade, hoping the opponent who wins it had only three spades and will be forced to return a diamond. As it happens, West will win and has nothing but diamonds left. He probably will lead a low diamond,

East will play the queen, and you win the king and land your contract by finessing the nine.

The defense could be clever and defeat you.

Can you see how?

East must keep all four of his spades and West must unblock by playing the queen and jack under the ace and king so the defense is in a position to cash two spades. Not many defenders find those plays.

Hand #4

North
♠ K Q 3 2
♥ K 8 5 2
♦ A Q 2
♣ 8 3

West
♠ 9 8
♥ Q 10 3
♦ 8 7 5
♣ K Q 10 7 2

East
♠ 10 5
♥ A 9 7
♦ J 10 9 6
♣ J 9 6 5

South
♠ A J 7 6 4
♥ J 6 4
♦ K 4 3
♣ A 4

CONTRACT: 4 ♠
OPENING LEAD: ♣K

You have a certain club loser and if each of your heart honors was captured by the ace and queen, you would have three heart losers—but no need for this. After winning the opening lead, pull trump which takes two rounds, cash your diamond winners, and feed them a club. A sluff and a ruff will allow you to pitch a heart from your hand and a heart lead will limit your heart losers to no more than two, regardless of the lie of the cards.

North
♠ A K 2
♥ A Q 10
♦ K Q 6
♣ A 8 5 4

South
♠ 6 3
♥ 7 3 2
♦ A 3 2
♣ K Q J 6 4

CONTRACT: 6 ♣
OPENING LEAD: ♦ J

After winning the diamond queen and pulling trump in three rounds, your contract is on ice. Play the ace and king of spades and trump a spade. Now play the king of diamonds and a diamond to the ace. You are ready for the heart suit. Lead small to the ten. If it loses to the jack, East will have to give you a free finesse or a sluff and a ruff.

Even if dummy had the nine of hearts instead of the ten, this play would work. If West inserted the ten, you would play the queen. If it lost to the king, East again would be end-played as only the jack is out and you have the ace and nine.

Sometimes you can *try* for an end play in a situation where if the right person happens to be on lead it would give you a trick. Note the following combinations:

1.	2.	3.	4.
A 2	A 3	K 4	A 5 4
Q 3	Q J	8 3	K J 6

1. If you have to lead this yourself, you have only one winner. Any time an opponent who holds the king leads this suit, you have two tricks.
2. Suppose you create a situation where an opponent must break this suit. If led from your left, you still can finesse as you would if you led it yourself. If led from your right, you are guaranteed two tricks.
3. Left to your own devices, you have a 50-50 chance of winning a trick. If RHO leads it, your chances are 100 percent.
4. Again you can lead to the jack for a 50-50 chance of an extra trick. If West leads the suit, you are at 100 percent.

Hand #6

North
♠ K 5 4
♥ J 10 3 2
♦ K 6 4
♣ K Q 5

West
♠ Q 10 2
♥ 9 8
♦ J 9 7 3
♣ 10 9 8 4

East
♠ A J 9 7 6
♥ A 6
♦ Q 10 5
♣ 7 6 3

South
♠ 8 3
♥ K Q 7 5 4
♦ A 8 2
♣ A J 2

CONTRACT: 4 ♥
OPENING LEAD: ♣ 10

After winning the club lead in hand, a trump is played which East wins. A club is returned and one more round of trump is played to clear the trump. Now what?

It simply costs nothing to play the last club followed by the king of diamonds, ace of diamonds and another diamond. If East wins the third diamond, you will not lose more than one spade as he is end-played. Yes, East could play the queen as you lead from the board towards your ace, but he may not, or, he may have started out with Q J 10.

There are many situations where you can try for this play, giving yourself an extra chance. If West wins, you have given nothing up. The ace of spades still could be placed favorably.

Becoming aware of this type of play also will be useful when you are defending. When you see it coming, you sometimes can avoid the end play, as in the last example.

XIII

INTRODUCTION TO SQUEEZES

A squeeze develops when one or both opponents have more than one suit they need to protect, and are forced to make so many discards they have to relinquish control of a critical suit. Most often it is exactly two suits an opponent is trying to protect.

When both opponents are squeezed it is called a DOUBLE SQUEEZE and when only one is being squeezed it is called a SIMPLE SQUEEZE or sometimes is referred to as a SINGLE SQUEEZE. The latter term is more descriptive since the word *simple* connotes "easy". A simple, or single, squeeze can be easy or it may be difficult.

Sometimes there is a choice of plays, i.e., taking a finesse or playing for a squeeze, but most of the time the contract has no hope except for the squeeze. **Typically, one must be able to win all but one of the available tricks for the squeeze to work.** A straight-forward example of a single squeeze is illustrated in the following hand:

Hand #1

North
♠ A K Q 6
♥ 8 6 2
♦ 10 8 6 2
♣ 6 4

South
♠ 7 5 3
♥ A J
♦ A
♣ A K Q J 9 7 5

CONTRACT: 7 ♣
OPENING LEAD: ♥ 10

East plays the heart queen and you win with the ace. You have 12 top winners and if the spades break 3-3, there are 13. There is one other possibility. You have all but one of the remaining tricks, so a squeeze could develop. You have played one card and have seven club tricks plus the ace of diamonds for a total of nine winners outside the spade suit. Think about what will happen as you cash those nine winners. If the hand that has the king of hearts also has four or more spades, he will be in a bind as he will have only four cards left so he cannot keep the king of hearts as well as four spades. He has no happy choice. If he parts with the heart king your jack will be good and if he parts with a spade, dummy's six will become a winner.

If you can look at a hand like this one and recognize what is needed to make this contract (other than a 3-3 spade break), you are on your way to understanding squeezes. The opposing hands were deliberately not given, because after the heart queen was played at trick one, the opposing hands can be any way you wish, as long as the hand that has the heart king also has four or more spades. Notice that for the squeeze to work, at least one of the possible winners or "threat cards" must be in the hand opposite the last of the winners you are cashing, AND there must be an entry to that card.

If a heart is not led at trick one, it is still right to cash all seven clubs and the red suit aces. If someone has the king **and** queen of hearts as well as four or more spades, he will be squeezed.

Because of the fact that opponents so often have discarding problems, when you have all but one of the remaining tricks, it is good technique to cash all of your winners before attacking the critical suit. In addition to legitimate problems, people will make errors when they have to make so many discards. For example, if someone has a diamond honor or a heart honor as well as four spades, he may discard a spade, thinking he must protect the honor. When a person only thinks he is being squeezed it is referred to as a psuedo squeeze. It works almost as often as a real one.

Hand #2

North
♠ A K Q 4
♥ 6 4 3 2
♦ 5 4 3
♣ 10 8

South
♠ 7 5
♥ A K 7 5
♦ A K Q J 9 7 6
♣ —

CONTRACT: 7 ♦
OPENING LEAD: ♣K

A small slam would have been a more reasonable contract, but you are in seven. You have 12 tricks, but unlike the last hand there is no possible way to make it unless someone has discarding problems. You have all but one of the winners, so the scene is ready for a squeeze. Figure out what you need for an opponent to have in his hand.

The situation is far from hopeless. Only one person can protect each of the major suits, so if the hand with four or more spades also has three or more hearts you will land the slam. This time the heart seven in your hand or dummy's small spade could become a winner.

You trump the opening lead, and you have six more trumps. After those seven cards are played, if one opponent holds the stopper for both major suits he can no longer hold on to the four spades and three hearts. Be sure to note, however, that you will have to count the hearts that are played so you will know if your little seven spot is a winner. If the heart isn't good, the spade will be if the conditions are as hoped.

The East-West hands could be as shown below, or reversed. The squeeze would work in either case.

West (or East)	East (or West)
♠ 10 8 6 2	♠ J 9 3
♥ J 10 9	♥ Q 8
♦ 10	♦ 8 2
♣ K Q 6 4 3	♣ A J 9 7 5 2

Hand #3

North
♠ 5 4
♥ 10 6 2
♦ A K Q 2
♣ A K Q 4

West
♠ 10 9 8
♥ 8
♦ J 10 8 5 3
♣ 10 8 7 3

East
♠ K Q J 7 3 2
♥ 9 7 4 3
♦ 9
♣ J 9

South
♠ A 6
♥ A K Q J 5
♦ 7 6 4
♣ 6 5 2

CONTRACT: 7NT
OPENING LEAD: ♠ 10

You have 12 top winners with a possible extra in either minor suit. If either minor splits 3-3 or if West holds four or more cards in both suits, he will be squeezed, but this hand doesn't quite play itself. If someone doesn't understand squeezes, but has been told to always run the long suit, he will run into an embarrassing situation on the last heart. On the fourth heart a spade could be discarded, but on the fifth heart, a small club or diamond must be discarded before knowing about the distribution of either suit.

If you play the top winners of either minor suit beginning at trick two, you will know if it splits 3-3. If not, notice what is the outstanding card or cards in that suit. Say you pick clubs to play first; as you play the third club, East will show out, so West holds the high club. Now as you run your hearts you can make a knowledgeable discard. If West keeps his high club you can throw yours away. Now you will make the hand if either minor splits 3-3 or if West has discarding problems, which he will in this case. After you played nine winners, a spade, three clubs and five hearts, West can't hold the high club as well as four diamonds.

Notice that in this case, when both potential winners or threat cards are in the same hand, only the opponent who has to discard before that hand can be squeezed. If East held length in both suits, he could make his decision *after* dummy.

Hand #4

North
♠ 8 4
♥ A K Q 2
♦ 10 9 6 4
♣ 6 4 2

West
♠ K Q J 6 3 2
♥ J 4
♦ 8 7 3 2
♣ 8

East
♠ 10 9 5
♥ 10 9 8 3
♦ 5
♣ J 10 9 5 3

South
♠ A 7
♥ 7 6 5
♦ A K Q J
♣ A K Q 7

CONTRACT: 6NT
OPENING LEAD: ♠K

You have 11 sure tricks which is within one of what you need, but two away from the number of tricks available. Refuse the first spade so you have all but one of the tricks at large. This play is referred to as RECTIFYING THE COUNT. Now, in addition to making the contract if either hearts or clubs are 3-3, you will make it if either opponent has four or more cards of the two suits.

Play the four diamonds and watch for club discards. If the last club is good, you have 12 tricks, if not, as the cards are, dummy's little heart will be a winner. You might try the hand without refusing the first spade. You will notice that East will not have a discarding problem unless you own all but one of the tricks available.

Hand #5

North
- ♠ A 4
- ♥ J 10 6 4
- ♦ A K Q 3
- ♣ 10 8 4

West
- ♠ J 8 6 2
- ♥ 8
- ♦ 10 6 4
- ♣ A 9 6 3 2

East
- ♠ K 10 9 3
- ♥ 9 7 5
- ♦ J 9 5 2
- ♣ 7 5

South
- ♠ Q 7 5
- ♥ A K Q 3 2
- ♦ 8 7
- ♣ K Q J

CONTRACT: 6 ♥
OPENING LEAD: ♣A

A spade lead would have made this hand pass quickly. You would play low, hoping West underled the king. Yes, people do underlead kings against slams. Sometimes it may be the only lead to beat the contract. Enough rambling. West led the ace of clubs and continued a club which you won. The opponents rectified the count for you as you have 11 winners and there are now 12 tricks at large. **Which are your two threat cards, what holding do you need for an opponent to have, and how do you exert the pressure?**

The queen of spades is the threat card in your hand, and the diamond four is the threat card in dummy. You need for one opponent to hold four or more diamonds and the king of spades. You must play off the ace of spades before running all of the winners in your hand to create this position:

North
- ♠ A 4
- ♥ J 10 6 4
- ♦ A K Q 3
- ♣ 10 8 4

South
- ♠ Q 7 5
- ♥ A K Q 3 2
- ♦ 8 7
- ♣ K Q J

This squeeze will work against either East or West, as either will be down to four cards and cannot keep the king of spades as well as four diamonds. This hand involves no counting at all: Just watch for the king of spades.

The playing off of the ace of spades early is called a VIENNA COUP: A fancy sounding name for a rather simple play. If this play were not made early, you wouldn't know what to discard from dummy on the last trump. After playing the ace of spades and the rest of your winners from your hand, the situation is actually the same as in hands #1 and #2. The lead is in your hand, which owns one threat card, and the other threat card is in dummy, with dummy having an entry. Either opponent can be squeezed.

In example three, only one opponent (West) could be squeezed. In the others, either could be squeezed, but only one would be. In the next example both will be squeezed. In the double squeeze, each opponent must be guarding one suit so neither can protect the third.

Hand #6

```
                    North
                    ♠ 8 6 5
                    ♥ 10 3
                    ♦ A Q J 6 5 4
                    ♣ 6 5

West                                    East
♠ K Q J 7 4 2                           ♠ 3
♥ 9 8 7 5 4                             ♥ Q J 6
♦ 10 7                                  ♦ 9 8
♣ —                                     ♣ Q J 10 9 8 7 2

                    South
                    ♠ A 10 9
                    ♥ A K 2
                    ♦ K 3 2
                    ♣ A K 4 3
```

THE AUCTION:

West	North	East	South
		3C	DBL
Pass	5D	Pass	6NT
Pass	Pass	Pass	

OPENING LEAD: ♠K

Having developed an awareness of squeeze play technique, you refuse the first trick as you have only 11 winners.

The spade queen is continued, East shows out, and you win the ace. West is now known to have the spade guard, and because of the preempt, East is known to have the club cards. Your threat cards are dummy's eight of spades (the 10 in your hand wouldn't work as on the running of the diamonds your hand pitches before West), and the club four and heart deuce in your hand. You must play all your winners except for the third suit which is hearts. Play the ace and king of clubs. Then run the diamonds. Watch for the jack of spades and *count* the clubs. As you are about to play the last diamond, the hand will look like this:

<pre>
                        North
                        ♠ 8 6 5
                        ♥ 10 3
                        ♦ A Q J 6 5 4
                        ♣ 6 5

West   East
♠ K Q J 7 4 2   ♠ 3
♥ 9 8 7 5 4   ♥ Q J 6
♦ 10 7   ♦ 9 8
♣ —   ♣ Q J 10 9 8 7 2

                        South
                        ♠ A 10 9
                        ♥ A K 2
                        ♦ K 3 2
                        ♣ A K 4 3
</pre>

As you play the last diamond, East either will have to play his last club, which would make your four good, or he will part with a heart as you throw your club. Now West either will play his spade jack which would make your eight good, or will part with a heart. If he chooses to play a heart, each opponent has only two hearts and your heart deuce is a winner!

Because of the magic-like quality of squeeze plays, many bridge players become fascinated with the subject. There are so many different types of squeezes or squeeze positions that the study of the subject is a separate hobby in itself. In bridge tournaments, some individuals are more interested in a particular hand which has a criss-cross squeeze or a transfer squeeze than they are in the outcome of the whole event.

You can play an excellent game of bridge with only a basic understanding of the subject. If, however, you wish to pursue it, there are several excellent books on squeezes available through bridge supply houses.

Plan your play on the following hands. Solutions on page 107.

Hand #1

North
- ♠ J 10 3
- ♥ 54
- ♦ A K 3 2
- ♣ J 6 5 4

South
- ♠ K Q
- ♥ A K Q J
- ♦ Q
- ♣ A Q 9 7 3 2

CONTRACT: 6 ♣
OPENING LEAD: ♠ A

    After winning the spade ace, West continues with a low spade to your king, East following.

Hand #2

North
- ♠ 10 9 8 7 3
- ♥ Q 10 2
- ♦ 7 3 2
- ♣ A Q

South
- ♠ K Q J 5 4 2
- ♥ 7 3
- ♦ A K 5
- ♣ K 4

CONTRACT: 4 ♠
OPENING LEAD: ♣ J

Hand #3

North
- ♠ A Q 3
- ♥ K 8 3
- ♦ K J 5
- ♣ A 9 6 2

South
- ♠ K 6 4 2
- ♥ A 6 4
- ♦ A Q 6 3 2
- ♣ 3

CONTRACT: 6 ♦
OPENING LEAD: ♣ K

Hand #4

North
- ♠ K 6 3
- ♥ A 8
- ♦ A 8 5 3
- ♣ A K 6 4

South
- ♠ A Q 2
- ♥ K J 4 3
- ♦ K Q 9 6 4
- ♣ 5

CONTRACT: 7 ♦
OPENING LEAD: ♣ J

Hand #5

North
- ♠ 10 4 3 2
- ♥ 8 6 5
- ♦ 7 6 3
- ♣ J 3 2

South
- ♠ A K J 8 7
- ♥ A K
- ♦ A Q J
- ♣ Q 7 4

CONTRACT: 4 ♠
OPENING LEAD: ♣K

After winning the club king, West switches to a heart.

Hand #6

North
- ♠ 10 9 8
- ♥ 8 6 4
- ♦ A K 9 2
- ♣ K J 7

South
- ♠ K Q J 6 4
- ♥ 5 3
- ♦ Q 5 3
- ♣ A 6 4

CONTRACT: 3 ♠
OPENING LEAD: ♥K

After West opens with one heart, your side competes to three spades which, if you make, will win the rubber. West leads the heart king, which draws the queen from East. West continues with a low heart. East wins with the ten and plays the jack.

Hand #7

North
- ♠ A 8 3
- ♥ A K Q 4
- ♦ K Q 3
- ♣ K 5 2

South
- ♠ Q
- ♥ 7 3 2
- ♦ A J 10 5 4 2
- ♣ J 6 4

CONTRACT: 6 ♦
OPENING LEAD: ♣ A

West continues with the spade jack.

Hand #8

North
- ♠ 7 5
- ♥ 6 5
- ♦ J 10 8 4 2
- ♣ A K 4 3

South
- ♠ A 8
- ♥ A Q 3
- ♦ 6
- ♣ Q J 10 8 7 5 2

CONTRACT: 5♣
3NT would have been easy but you landed in 5♣.
OPENING LEAD: ♦3

East wins the diamond lead with the ace and switches to the heart jack. You insert the queen, which loses to the king and another heart is returned.

Hand #9

North
- ♠ K 8 6 4
- ♥ 8 3
- ♦ A K J 3
- ♣ 6 3 2

South
- ♠ A
- ♥ A K Q 1 0 5 2
- ♦ 7 5 2
- ♣ 8 5 4

CONTRACT: 4 ♥
OPENING LEAD: ♣K

West cashes his three high clubs as all follow, then switches to the spade ten. You win the ace and play two high trump. On the second trump, West discards a spade.

Hand #10

North
- ♠ K 6
- ♥ 7 6 4
- ♦ A K 5 4
- ♣ K J 3 2

South
- ♠ A 7 3 2
- ♥ A K Q
- ♦ Q J 6
- ♣ A 8 4

CONTRACT: 6NT
OPENING LEAD: ♥10

Hand #11

North
- ♠ 1 0 9 3 2
- ♥ K 7 4
- ♦ 5 3 2
- ♣ A 1 0 2

South
- ♠ K Q J 6 4
- ♥ A 2
- ♦ A 6 4
- ♣ K 9 3

CONTRACT: 4 ♠
OPENING LEAD: ♥Q

After winning the heart lead in hand, you play the spade king. East wins and returns another heart.

Hand #12

North
- ♠ K 3 2
- ♥ 8 5 4
- ♦ K 6 3
- ♣ 7 5 3 2

South
- ♠ A 9 6
- ♥ A Q 1 0 7 3 2
- ♦ A 7
- ♣ 9 8

THE AUCTION

West	North	East	South
1C	Pass	Pass	2H
Pass	3H	Pass	4H

OPENING LEAD: ♣K

East overtakes his partner's king with the ace and returns a club. West Wins the ten and plays the club queen as East discards a diamond.

Hand #13

North
- ♠ A Q J
- ♥ Q 9 4 2
- ♦ 8 7 5
- ♣ Q J 2

South
- ♠ 4
- ♥ A K 8 7 6 3
- ♦ A 6
- ♣ 7 6 5 4

THE AUCTION

South	West	North	East
			Pass
1H	Pass	3H	Pass
4H	Pass	Pass	Pass

OPENING LEAD: ♣10

You play the club jack, East wins the king and switches to the diamond queen. You win the ace and play the ace and king of hearts. West follows small on the first and discards a small spade on the second.

Hand #14

North
- ♠ Q J 7 2
- ♥ K 6
- ♦ A Q 9
- ♣ A 8 6 4

South
- ♠ A K 8 6 3
- ♥ A 7 4
- ♦ 6 5 4
- ♣ K 2

CONTRACT: ♠6

OPENING LEAD: ♣9

You win the club king, and play the ace and king of trump as both follow.

Hand #15

North
- ♠ 8 7 5 2
- ♥ J 8 3
- ♦ K 9 4
- ♣ J 5 4

South
- ♠ Q 6 4
- ♥ A K Q 7 6 2
- ♦ A 5 2
- ♣ A

THE AUCTION

West	North	East	South
	Pass	3C	4H
Pass	Pass	Pass	

OPENING LEAD: ♠ K

The king of spades is followed by the ace as East discards a club. A low spade is continued which East ruffs. East returns the club king.

Solution to quiz hands:

Hand #1

North
- ♠ J 10 3
- ♥ 5 4
- ♦ A K 3 2
- ♣ J 6 5 4

West
- ♠ A 8 7 5 4 2
- ♥ 10 3 2
- ♦ 8 7 5 4
- ♣ —

East
- ♠ 9 6
- ♥ 9 8 7 6
- ♦ J 10 9 6
- ♣ K 10 8

South
- ♠ K Q
- ♥ A K Q J
- ♦ Q
- ♣ A Q 9 7 3 2

Overtake the diamond queen with the king and lead the club jack. This is one of those rare cases in which it is right to lead the jack although you don't have the ten. If it's covered, win the ace, play two top hearts and trump the third to take the marked finesse against the trump ten.

Hand #2

North
- ♠ 10 9 8 7 3
- ♥ Q 10 2
- ♦ 7 3 2
- ♣ A Q

West
- ♠ 6
- ♥ A J 6 5
- ♦ 9 6 4
- ♣ J 10 9 3 2

East
- ♠ A
- ♥ K 9 8 4
- ♦ Q J 10 8
- ♣ 8 7 6 5

South
- ♠ K Q J 5 4 2
- ♥ 7 3
- ♦ A K 5
- ♣ K 4

Win the club in hand and lead a heart to the ten immediately. If a diamond is returned, win in hand and lead another heart towards the queen. The heart trick must be established before the opponents have a chance to knock out the ace and king of diamonds and collect their diamond trick.

North
- ♠ A Q 3
- ♥ K 8 3
- ♦ K J 5
- ♣ A 9 6 2

West
- ♠ J 10 7 5
- ♥ J 7 5
- ♦ 10 8
- ♣ K Q J 5

East
- ♠ 9 8
- ♥ Q 10 9 2
- ♦ 9 7 4
- ♣ 10 8 7 4

South
- ♠ K 6 4 2
- ♥ A 6 4
- ♦ A Q 6 3 2
- ♣ 3

Win the club ace and ruff a club follow by the ace and then king of diamonds. If both follow, things look bright. Ruff another club, play a spade to the ace and ruff your last club. Now play a heart to the king and pull the last trump.

If someone were to show out as you played the second round of trump, you would abandon the dummy reversal and hope for a 3-3 spade break (or that a squeeze would develop).

Hand #4

North
♠ K 6 3
♥ A 8
♦ A 8 5 3
♣ A K 6 4

West
♠ 10 7 5 4
♥ Q 10 6 2
♦ —
♣ J 10 8 7 2

East
♠ J 9 8
♥ 9 7 5
♦ J 10 7 2
♣ Q 9 3

South
♠ A Q 2
♥ K J 4 3
♦ K Q 9 6 4
♣ 5

Play the ace of diamonds at trick two, as you can handle four cards in the East hand. When you discover the 4-0 break, lead a trump and cover whatever East plays. Play the ace and king of hearts, ruff a heart and lead another diamond.

Hand #5

North
♠ 10 4 3 2
♥ 8 6 5
♦ 7 6 3
♣ J 3 2

West
♠ Q 9 5
♥ J 10 7 3
♦ 8 5
♣ A K 9 5

East
♠ 6
♥ Q 9 4 2
♦ K 10 9 4 2
♣ 10 8 6

South
♠ A K J 8 7
♥ A K
♦ A Q J
♣ Q 7 4

Play the queen under the king of clubs. West almost certainly has the ace, so your jack will be a third round winner. If you have a spade loser you will need two entries to dummy for the diamond finesses. If you don't unblock the club queen, you could be prevented from winning a club in dummy. (Also, the play of the club queen may cause West to switch suits if he has five of them and could give his partner a ruff).

Hand #6

North
♠ 10 9 8
♥ 8 6 4
♦ A K 9 2
♣ K J 7

West
♠ A 7 5 2
♥ A K 9 7 2
♦ J 10
♣ 9 3

East
♠ 3
♥ Q J 10
♦ 8 7 6 5
♣ Q 10 8 5 2

South
♠ K Q J 6 4
♥ 5 3
♦ Q 5 3
♣ A 6 4

If you trump it, the contract will fail. West will win the *third* round of trump and lead another heart, which will take your last trump while he still has one left. When he wins it you can't cope with another heart return. Since you are only in three, discard a small club from your hand. Now the trump holding in your hand can't be shortened as dummy can handle a heart continuation.

Hand #7

North
- ♠ A 8 3
- ♥ A K Q 4
- ♦ K Q 3
- ♣ K 5 2

West
- ♠ J 10 9 4 2
- ♥ 9 8
- ♦ 9 8 7 6
- ♣ A 7

East
- ♠ K 7 6 5
- ♥ J 10 6 5
- ♦ —
- ♣ Q 10 9 8 3

South
- ♠ Q
- ♥ 7 3 2
- ♦ A J 10 5 4 2
- ♣ J 6 4

Play the ace of spades and pull trump, pitching a spade. **Play the king of clubs**, then ruff a spade to your hand and play the last two trumps, watching for the club queen. Either opponent (in this case East) will be squeezed if he started out with the club queen as well as four or more hearts.

North
- ♠ 7 5
- ♥ 6 5
- ♦ J 10 8 4 2
- ♣ A K 4 3

West
- ♠ Q 9 3 2
- ♥ K 8 7 2
- ♦ K 7 5 3
- ♣ 9

East
- ♠ K J 10 6 4
- ♥ J 10 9 4
- ♦ A Q 9
- ♣ 6

South
- ♠ A 8
- ♥ A Q 3
- ♦ 6
- ♣ Q J 10 8 7 5 2

After winning the heart ace, play the club five to the king, trump a diamond high and lead a high trump to the ace and trump another diamond high. Lead the club *deuce* to the three and trump one more diamond. Your last diamond is now good, which will take care of your spade loser. You can get to dummy one last time by ruffing a heart.

Hand #9

North
- ♠ K 8 6 4
- ♥ 8 3
- ♦ A K J 3
- ♣ 6 3 2

West
- ♠ J 10 9 5 2
- ♥ 9
- ♦ Q 6 4
- ♣ A K Q 7

East
- ♠ Q 7 3
- ♥ J 7 6 4
- ♦ 10 9 8
- ♣ J 10 9

South
- ♠ A
- ♥ A K Q 10 5 2
- ♦ 7 5 2
- ♣ 8 5 4

The diamond finesse is not necessary as far as side suit losers, but is mandatory as an entry to dummy. Lead a diamond to the jack, ruff a spade, lead a diamond to the king, ruff a spade and lead your last diamond to the ace. Now as you lead either remaining card from dummy, East is trapped.

Hand #10

North
♠ K 6
♥ 7 6 4
♦ A K 5 4
♣ K J 3 2

West
♠ Q 8 4
♥ 10 9 8 5
♦ 8 3
♣ 10 9 7 6

East
♠ J 10 9 5
♥ J 3 2
♦ 10 9 7 2
♣ Q 5

South
♠ A 7 3 2
♥ A K Q
♦ Q J 6
♣ A 8 4

Play the king followed by the ace of clubs. The safety play is called for as you need only one extra club trick. The chance of getting a third club trick is over 75% (See Ch. XI, Ex. #9).

Hand #11

North
- ♠ 10 9 3 2
- ♥ K 7 4
- ♦ 5 3 2
- ♣ A 10 2

West
- ♠ A 5
- ♥ Q J 10 3
- ♦ J 9 7
- ♣ J 8 7 4

East
- ♠ 8 7
- ♥ 9 8 6 5
- ♦ K Q 10 8
- ♣ Q 6 5

South
- ♠ K Q J 6 4
- ♥ A 2
- ♦ A 6 4
- ♣ K 9 3

You win the king, pull trump ending in dummy and ruff a heart. Now play the ace of diamonds and a diamond. Whoever wins can cash one more diamond, but next will have to break the club suit or give you a sluff and a ruff.

Hand #12

North
- ♠ K 3 2
- ♥ 8 5 4
- ♦ K 6 3
- ♣ 7 5 3 2

West
- ♠ Q J 7 4
- ♥ K
- ♦ Q J 2
- ♣ K Q J 10 6

East
- ♠ 10 8 5
- ♥ J 9 6
- ♦ 10 9 8 5 4
- ♣ A 4

South
- ♠ A 9 6
- ♥ A Q 10 7 3 2
- ♦ A 7
- ♣ 9 8

You have a spade to lose in addition to the two clubs, so you can't afford any trump losers. RHO has shown up with the ace of clubs and didn't respond to his partner's one club opening. It is a near certainty he doesn't own the king of hearts. Your only hope, therefore, is a singleton king in the opening bidder's hand. After ruffing the third club, play the ace of hearts. When the king drops go to the board and take the marked finesse against the jack.

Hand #13

North
- ♠ A Q J
- ♥ Q 9 4 2
- ♦ 8 7 5
- ♣ Q J 2

West
- ♠ K 9 7 6 2
- ♥ 5
- ♦ K 10 4 3
- ♣ 10 9 8

East
- ♠ 10 5 4 3
- ♥ J 10
- ♦ Q J 9 2
- ♣ A K 3

South
- ♠ 4
- ♥ A K 8 7 6 3
- ♦ A 6
- ♣ 7 6 5 4

From the lead and play to the first trick, East is presumed to have the ace and king of clubs. His return of the diamond queen indicates the jack of diamonds and he had the heart jack. This gives him 11 HCP so he cannot have the spade king as well since he didn't open the bidding. Play the ace and king of trump and take a straight finesse in the spade suit. The ace will provide a parking place for the losing diamond.

Hand #14

North
♠ Q J 7 2
♥ K 6
♦ A Q 9
♣ A 8 6 4

West
♠ 10 4
♥ J 9 5 3 2
♦ J 7 3 2
♣ 9 7

East
♠ 9 5
♥ Q 10 8
♦ K 10 8
♣ Q J 10 5 3

South
♠ A K 8 6 3
♥ A 7 4
♦ 6 5 4
♣ K 2

Play the ace of clubs and ruff a club. Now the king of hearts, ace of hearts, ruff a heart and ruff another club. Both your hand and dummy will have one trump left and three diamonds. Lead a diamond to the nine. East will win the ten and is end-played. It would do no good for West to play the jack as you lead the diamond as you would play the queen. East could win the king, but again would be end-played.

Hand #15

North
♠ 8 7 5 2
♥ J 8 3
♦ K 9 4
♣ J 5 4

West
♠ A K 10 9 3
♥ 10 5 4
♦ Q 10 6
♣ 8 7

East
♠ J
♥ 9
♦ J 8 7 3
♣ K Q 10 9 6 3 2

South
♠ Q 6 4
♥ A K Q 7 6 2
♦ A 5 2
♣ A

You have lost three tricks and still have a diamond loser. The good news is you have all but one of the remaining winners, and West is known to have the remaining spades winners and East almost certainly has the club queen (from the bidding as well as his lead).

As you run your hearts, count the spades (or watch for the ten and nine). As you play the sixth heart, if the eight of spades isn't good, discard it. Ten cards will have been played, so if West discards the high spades, your eight will be good, and if he keeps a high spade, he can have no more than two diamonds. Assuming he kept the spade, dummy will have the king and nine of diamonds plus the jack of clubs. East will have the same problem as West, as he will need to keep the club queen or your jack will be good, so he can have no more than two diamonds. Play a diamond to dummy's king and the nine to the ace. The five of diamonds will be a winner.

TABLE OF OPENING LEADS

Given that the choice of which suit to lead has been selected, the following are standard leads.

	Versus no-trump	Versus suit
K8652	5	5
KQ862	6	K
KQJ63	K	K
KJ1084	J	J
KQ1094	K (Note 1)	K
Q8632	3	3
QJ1064	Q	Q
QJ964	Q	Q
QJ752	5	Q
J9632	3	3
J10942	J	J
J10542	4	J or 4
109862	10	10
108742	4	4
AKQ64	K	K
AKJ104	A (Note 2)	K
A97652	6	A
AJ1094	J	A
A109864	10	A
A9874	7	A
K964	4	4
K987	7	7
1098	10	10
A73	3	A
QJ6	Q (Note 3)	Q
Q74	4	4
J103	J	J
J84	4	4
1092	10	10
1063	3	3
974	9	9
763	7	7
A2	A	A
94	9	9
J6	J	J

Note 1: Many play that the lead of the queen asks for partner to unblock the jack.

Note 2: Asks for partner to unblock the queen.

Note 3: Though not a sequence, the queen is led because if this is partner's suit it may be necessary to unblock

A Few Generalizations

—With doubletons the higher card is led.

—The top card is led from sequences or near sequences. A sequence is defined as three or more touching cards of which at least one of them is an honor, 1098 being the lowest sequence. J108xx is an example of a near sequence.

—Versus suit contracts, the upper card is usually led from touching honors except that the king is led from AKxxx.

—Aces are not underled against suit contracts. As a rule, suits with aces (assuming the king is not present) are not led at all unless 1) partner had bid the suit, 2) you have a singleton or a doubleton and are hoping to get a ruff, and 3) you have a long suit so that partner may get a ruff. In all cases, if leading the suit, lead the ace, not low.

—Lead fourth best from broken holdings such as J9752 against either no trump or suit.

—If partner has bid, lead his suit unless there is a very good reason for another lead.

TABLE OF PERCENTAGES

The following table indicates the likelihood of specific distributions of the opponents cards. The information is most relevant when your side owns length in the suit, so the table begins with your side having six or more. The numbers have been rounded off.

Your side has	Cards missing	Division of opponent's cards	Percentage
6	(7)	4-3	62 %
		5-2	30 %
		6-1	7 %
		7-0	0.5%
7	(6)	4-2	48 %
		3-3	36 %
		5-1	15 %
		6-0	1 %
8	(5)	3-2	68 %
		4-1	28 %
		5-0	4 %
9	(4)	3-1	50 %
		2-2	40 %
		4-0	10 %
10	(3)	2-1	78 %
		3-0	22 %
11	(2)	1-1	52 %
		2-0	48 %

A fairly easy way of figuring the odds is to list all the possible distributions which can exist and count the number of any particular one to arrive at a ratio. This procedure isn't 100% accurate due to the fact that there is a limited number of cards one is working with rather than an infinite number, but it is close enough to be practical.

Take the example of four cards outstanding. Say the four cards are Q 4 3 2. The possible combinations are these:

Left:	Right:
3 2	Q 4
4 2	Q 3
4 3	Q 2
Q 4	2 3
Q 3	2 4
Q 2	2 3
Q 3 2	4
Q 4 2	3
Q 4 3	2
4 3 2	Q
4	Q 3 2
3	Q 4 2
2	Q 4 3
Q	4 3 2
Q 4 3 2	—
—	Q 4 3 2

There is a quick check to determine if you have missed any of the possibilities: 2 to the power of the number of cards you are missing will give the total number of combinations. In this example, 2 to the 4th power = 16 possible combinations. There are eight combinations of 3-1 breaks, so 8/16 or 50% is the approximate likelihood of a 3-1 break. The inaccuracy mentioned previously becomes pronounced in the 4-0 break. That occurs 2/16 of the time which is 12.5%. However, with only thirteen cards in each hand, the percentages level out somewhat, meaning the extreme breaks will occur a bit less often.

For those interested in the exact percentages, the formula for putting "r" objects into "n" slots is:

$$\frac{n!}{r!(n-r)!}$$

Should you have missed or forgotten this from your math, "!", which is called a factorial, means multiplying all the numbers from one to the number. 5! would be 1x2x3x4x5 or 120. With this example,

$$\frac{7!}{5!}$$

you could cancel out the 5! and would have,

$$\frac{1\times2\times3\times4\times5\textbf{x6x7}}{1\times2\times3\times4\times5} \text{ or } 42$$

The chance of any one of 26 cards being in one of 13 slots is an obvious 1 out of 2, but notice how the formula works so you can apply it in more complex situations:

(n = slots, r = objects)

$$\frac{\text{one object being in one of 13 slots}}{\text{divided by total number of slots and objects (26,2)}}$$

Plugging the numbers into the formula of both the numberator and denominator we get:

$$\frac{\dfrac{13!}{1!(12!)}}{\dfrac{26!}{1!(25!)}} = \frac{13}{26} = \frac{1}{2}$$

Now if we want to calculate a 3-1 break, we are considering the division of 4 of the 26 cards and figuring the chance of one of those four cards being in one of the thirteen slots at the same time as the other 3 cards are in the other group of 13. Using the formula, we get:

$$\frac{\text{1 slot, 13 objects times* 3 slots, 13 objects}}{\text{divided by total number of slots and objects (26,4)}}$$

*the chance of both occuring at the same time must be multiplied, not added.

$$\frac{\dfrac{13!}{1!(12!)} \quad x \quad \dfrac{13!}{3!(10!)}}{\dfrac{26!}{4!(22!)}} = 0.249$$

This calculates only one of the 3-1 breaks, so it is necessary to multiply by 2 to allow for the 3-1 in the opposite hands, so we have:

$$0.249 \times 2 = 0.498 = 49.8\%$$

The probability of a 4-0 break would be calculated as follows:

$$\frac{\text{0 objects falling into one of 13 slots times 4 objects}}{\text{falling into 13 slots}} \times 2$$
$$\text{divided by the total number of slots and objects}$$

Using the formula, we have,

(Note: 0! is defined as 1)

$$\frac{\dfrac{13!}{0!(13!)} \quad x \quad \dfrac{13!}{4!(9!)}}{\dfrac{26!}{4!(22!)}} \times 2$$

or,

$$\frac{715}{14950} \times 2 = 0.096, \text{ or } 9.6\%$$